HEALTH CARE CONSTITUTIONS

Diane Longley, LLB, MA
Faculty of Law
University of Sheffield

Cavendish
Publishing
Limited

First published in Great Britain 1996 by Cavendish Publishing Limited, The Glass House, Wharton Street, London, WC1X 9PX.
Telephone: 0171-278 8000   Facsimile: 0171-278 8080

British Library Cataloguing in Publication Data

Longley, D
Health Care Constitutions
(Medico-Legal Series)
I. Title II. Series
361.1

ISBN 1-85941-020-0

Printed and bound in Great Britain

PREFACE

This book is primarily concerned with the dilemmas and lack of public confidence which are currently apparent in the National Health Service. In seeking to suggest what might have contributed to these difficulties the organisation and delivery of health care in the United Kingdom, Canada and New Zealand are compared and contrasted from the point of view of choice and public accountability. An analysis is made of the philosophies underlying the reforms being undertaken in each country to see if constitutional expectations are being met.

Considerable changes are taking place in the delivery of public services throughout the developed world. Government at both central and local levels in many countries is in a state of flux. Traditional government functions and services are being contracted out, marketised or privatised. This is giving rise to a multitude of conceptual and practical difficulties. In health care systems the issues that arise in accountability and choice are in many ways a manifestation of the inherent and complex network of relationships. The focus of concern, with which all countries are grappling is governance in its broadest and most democratic sense. This is in essence a constitutional matter, the backbone of which is the need to ensure that our underlying and enduring values will influence the choices made about objectives and the means available to attain them. In a world where expectation and demand for public services is as high as the desire to contain costs, the task has been to thoroughly assess old ways and search for new ways of government which, in the light of present circumstance, will deliver services in a manner which accords to constitutional commitments.

Each country is tackling its problems in different ways, although the aims and the problems are similar in each. Given their different constitutional and organisational backgrounds is there any common ground for reform? What mistakes are being made? Is there anything that we can learn from Canada and New Zealand to solve our difficulties?

Diane Longley
March 1996

iii

CONTENTS

CONTENTS

CHAPTER 1

FIRST PRINCIPLES

HEALTH

It is hardly necessary to state that health is universally recognised as an essential good. The constitution of the World Health Organisation (WHO) defines health as a:

> state of physical, mental and social well-being and not merely the absence of disease or infirmity.

This may undoubtedly be an ideal to which to aspire, but it underlines health as an integral part of what individuals need in order to realise their full potential and derive satisfaction from life. Rather than an end in itself health is a *means* towards the fulfilment of the latent possibilities of us all and a means of ensuring an acceptable quality of life. In other words, health is axiomatic to human development. In these terms, health is placed inextricably at the heart of social and economic concerns.[1]

The idea of health as a social responsibility rather than a merely personal one has become deeply embedded in the inner consciousness of many countries. The World Health Organisation (WHO) too, has recognised that responsibility for health cannot lie solely with the individual and that health matters warrant government attention:

> Governments have a responsibility for the health of their peoples which can be fulfilled only by the provision of adequate health and social measures.

Closer to home, Article 129 of the 1992 Treaty of European Union (the Maastricht Treaty) exhorts Member States of the European Community to take responsibility for developing a co-ordinated public health policy:

> The Community shall contribute towards ensuring a high level of human health protection by encouraging co-operation between Member States and if necessary lending support to their action.
>
> Community action shall be directed towards the prevention of diseases, in particular major health scourges, including drug dependence, by promoting research into their causes and their transmission as well as health information and education.

---

1   By Agenda 21 of the 1992 Rio Conference a number of governments committed themselves to a blueprint for a shift towards sustainable development which includes a chapter on the protection and promotion of health.

What is more, health protection requirements are to form a constituent part of other Community policies.[2] This is a clear acknowledgment that some of the most significant health gains have come about as a result of improvements in environmental conditions and nutrition rather than any direct intervention provided by the health services.

However, whilst the promotion and maintenance of good health is recognised to be a fundamental and legitimate policy objective for governments to pursue, there is scant guidance on the actual responsibilities and provision of health services which remain one of the most problematic of government functions. Governments have sought there own solutions and there are considerable differences in the organisational structure of health services throughout developed nations. However, despite these differences, the arrival of the 1990s has heralded a period of instability over much of the health care field. Health care activity in many countries has thus come under increasing scrutiny in recent years. Although escalating cost is for the most part a major catalyst for much of the development that is taking place, as governments seek to control public spending, increasing awareness that health care resources may frequently be being allocated on neither an optimal nor equitable basis, is also influencing the process of change.

Essentially, the allocation of health care resources raises complex ethical issues as well as social and economic difficulties and poses a challenge not only to those directly involved in health care but to the public at large. Fundamentally the question is one of the distribution of decision-making power for what have aptly been termed 'tragic choices'.[3] The dilemma is acknowledged by the WHO which has stated that by the year 2000 all Member States should have mechanisms in place to strengthen ethical considerations in decisions relating to the health of individuals, groups and populations.[4] Indeed some of the most controversial ethical debates of the last decade have focused on the problematic issue of how limited resources might be justly distributed and the nature of a health care system which will achieve that end. In what follows, it will be argued that whilst the means by which health care is delivered is contingent, the input that citizens

---

2   Though not yet widely appreciated, these provisions are likely to have a major impact on health policy-making in the United Kingdom. Priorities for European Union (EU) action are health promotion, education and training, health data and indicators, monitoring and surveillance of disease, cancer, drugs, AIDS and other communicable diseases, intentional and unintentional accidents and injuries, pollution related illness and rare diseases.

3   B Guy Peters, 'Tragic Choices: Rulemaking and Policy Choice' (1993) in *Ethics in Public Service* (R Chapman Ed).

4   *Targets for Health for All. The Health Policy for Europe* (WHO, 1991).

should have into the choices that are made as regards health policy and the allocation of resources is not.

PUBLIC SECTOR REFORM

At the outset it should be noted that the developments that are occurring in many health services throughout the western world ought not to be seen in isolation; rather they should be examined in the context of changes that are currently taking place within public services as a whole. These changes are tending to display a fairly similar pattern throughout a number of countries in that the role of government is being redefined at both central and local levels. To varying degrees and in varying manners government functions are being reassessed and restructured. This public sector reform, of a kind that is now almost universally characterised as New Public Management (NPM), has been proceeding swiftly. This is particularly so in the United Kingdom and New Zealand, but is also apparent in Canada, Australia and the USA. The central tenets of this new approach are: the driving downwards of responsibility for decision-making; the separation of policy making structures from service delivery systems; the increasing use of the private sector for delivery of public services; the setting of performance targets and service indicators and a greater emphasis on the quality of services delivered to the citizen in their capacity as a consumer.[5]

Allied to this has been the extension of contract as the vehicle which underpins the delivery of many public services and the development within the public sector of quasi-markets. The momentum towards pro-competitive market mimicking strategies is seen as the optimum means of containing cost and increasing efficiency, as well as improving quality and consumer choice. It is believed that these moves will stimulate the development of economic incentives and organisational capabilities, that will highlight and in turn lead to the limitation of unnecessary elements of public services and foster a more innovative delivery of those that remain.

At the heart of all these developments, the issue with which all countries are grappling, is 'the art of governance'; the search for a means of sharing public power which will lead to an efficient and just allocation of finite resources. The 'marketisation' of public services of which we are presently seeing so much can take to a lesser or greater extent one or more forms of policy intervention. These may include

---

5   N Lewis, 'Responsibility in Government: the Strange Case of the United Kingdom' (1995) *European Public Law* Vol 1:3.

privatisation, changes in regulation, charging for services, the introduction of elements of competition through contracting out or internal tendering and contract arrangements, or partnerships between the public and private sectors.

Even though the various forms of marketisation may be proceeding rapidly, the necessity for the conduct of government business is unlikely to diminish. On the contrary, the need for management of public matters has in all likelihood increased through the introduction of these new and varying forms for channelling government functions, the concerns, interests and the diversity of public organisations, their interdependence and networks of influence. Indeed stable democracy requires institutions which are intermediate between central government and the public. In effect, it can be argued that the introduction of elements of marketisation to public organisations has merely redefined the requirements of both government and management of public services and consequently choice and public accountability.[6]

This is perhaps a recognition that in a modern economy, planning in any real cognitive sense has become a virtual impossibility,[7] and the role of the state is to set broad strategies to encourage multiple competitive providers to determine delivery mechanisms and provide innovative solutions to perceived problems. In the now often repeated words of Osborne and Gaebler; the role of government is to 'steer not row'.[8] The need for adaptive mechanisms of public service management and complementary appropriate processes for legitimacy of decisions taken and choices made, are therefore in all probability even stronger.

Essentially, these are constitutional matters, the nub of concern is the need to ensure that our underlying and enduring values will direct the choices that are made and the means available to attain them. But as solutions and strategies are being sought a whole multitude of conceptual as well as practical difficulties are being highlighted and we need to consider carefully whether the rhetoric and reality of many of the developments currently taking place are actually sufficiently aligned to meet the expectations of fundamental constitutional beliefs.

The analysis put forward in this book is not that the difficulties stem from the use, *per se*, of market mechanisms and consumer sovereignty as the elements in which public sector reforms, including health, have been grounded. On the contrary, there is nothing

---

6   Metcalfe and Richards, *Improving Public Management* (1987).

7   N Lewis, *How to Reinvent British Government* (1993) European Policy Forum.

8   Osborne and Gaebler, *Reinventing Government* (1992).

inherently wrong with markets or market allied strategies. It can be argued that the very justification of the existence of markets is freedom of expression or choice, principles which also form the cornerstone of our commitments to human rights and consequent constitutional protections.[9] From this perspective markets and health are means to achieve a similar end, that of freedom and well-being.

The point is rather that our commitment to human rights and constitutional principles requires that where choice is failing to be sufficiently facilitated by the public service structures that have been put in place, the balance must be redressed. Consequently there needs to be an assessment of any tension that exists between the constitutional and political fields; and a re-adjustment of any misalignment between our founding values and underlying expectations on the one hand, and the means by which they are delivered on the other. Thus, constitutional beliefs should be the driving force of all governance, in what ever manner the latter manifests itself. In the United Kingdom the implications of this have not yet been thoroughly thought through, and whilst there are some innovative developments, our current system of checks and balances, our public law, is likely to struggle with the constitutional dilemmas posed today by the transition to the new management of public services.

HEALTH SERVICE REFORM

The apparent disarray and dichotomies of health care should not then be seen merely as the result of short-term difficulties, the issues are more deep seated than that. The current flux in health care is influenced by a series of deeply rooted political, social and economic forces that have combined to generate essentially similar needs for change throughout public services, regardless of any particular health sector difficulties.[10]

However, the sheer scale and diversity of the services required in the health care field, the continual development of new and highly technical procedures for diagnosis and treatment, not to mention the toll of ever increasing demand, have exerted specific recurrent pressures on health systems which have led to severe problems in

---

9   N Lewis, 'Markets Regulation and Citizenship; a Constitutional Analysis' (1993) in *Law and the Public Interest* (R Brownsword Ed).

10   R B Saltman and C von Otter, *Planned Markets and Public Competition; strategic reform of Northern European health systems* (Open University Press, 1992).

sustaining or even attaining their primary objectives. As expectation in health care has expanded so has the outlay.

In addition, there are a number of difficulties that arise in the health care sector that are in many ways a manifestation of the inherent and complex network of relationships that exist within the field itself and between health and other public policy areas. Health care is a major economic activity bound up with a significant proportion of gross domestic product. It is therefore inevitable that health care needs have to be considered alongside a wide range of other public and commercial policy matters. In the UK, Canada and New Zealand there have been continual problems with the overall planning and co-ordination of services. Not surprisingly, 'medical inflation' combined with the factors just described has caused governments to take a hard look at health care arrangements and seek more efficient use of resources in an effort to secure 'value for money'.

The conceptual and practical problems evolving in health care systems are now leading to organisational and structural changes which are profoundly affecting health service provision and are also challenging long held beliefs and practices amongst key stakeholders. But in the midst of these changes, before any satisfactory vision of the future can be developed, it is perhaps important to take stock, to consider what are the aspirations of a health system and to check out the forces that may be influencing and shaping fundamental choices. Once these 'first base' matters are addressed the possibilities for a health care system might then be better understood. Only then can a realisation or adjustment of expectations be worked towards through the setting of realistic objectives and the development of a framework suitable for their attainment.

THE ESSENCE OF CHOICE AND THE ROLE OF THE CONSTITUTION

The philosophy, or at least the rhetorical justification that underpins many of the current changes to the public sector, including health both at home and abroad is that of user choice.[11] Much of the health service reforms in the UK were predicated on enhanced local decision-making.[12] Most recently, the National Health Service (NHSE) Executive in its *Priorities and Planning Guidance for the NHS* (1995/6) has reiterated

---

11 This may be expressed in a number of different ways, consumer sovereignty, local decision-making, citizen empowerment but essentially the concept is the same.

12 Working for Patients (1989, Cmnd 555).

the need to develop a 'patient centred NHS' by requiring, as one of six medium term priorities, that health authorities give:

> greater voice and emphasis to users of NHS services and their carers in their own care, the development and definition of standards set for NHS services locally and the development of NHS policy both locally and nationally.

This is all to the good. A far more open, user responsive service has long been advocated. Over 20 years ago it was suggested that in the health service there should be:

> acceptance of the responsibility publicly to explain and justify policies, to welcome rather than stifle discussion of priorities and objectives, awareness of and sensitivity to public needs and a willingness to remedy errors.[13]

Such a focus implies that the public will be enabled readily to exercise their preferences in relation to the provision of health services, and that decisions will be justified by reflecting the values of those people most affected. Where this is not the case, decisions will be open to challenge. It also suggests that machinery will be provided to allow involvement of relevant parties in policy choices at a stage before decisions become irrevocable. The twin tenets here therefore are choice and accountability. But, for the most part, the 'sound bites' of enhanced choice tend to be more apparent than are any explanations of the means by which, or to what degree, it may be exercised. Certainly in the UK many of the arrangements for the realisation of user choice are such that a shift has evolved that has marginalised collective avenues for choice and has instead tended to emphasise an individual 'consumerist' perspective.

This individualist perspective, of course, fits with the common formula of NPM which emphasises individual responsibility, espouses a reduction of the role of the state, and exhorts the use of markets and competition for the provision of public services. The ideology is that through the provision of an element of competition in the delivery of public services citizens are able to exercise their choice in the marketplace. As citizens exit or 'vote with their feet', providers of public services will consequently strive to respond more effectively to the preferences displayed and improvements in quality will follow.

This approach is clearly one that has been overlooked for far too long in the field of public services, but the question is whether the initiatives which are now being put in place address the *full* extent of the nature of choice within the public arena and the relationship between choice and the broader social enterprise.

---

13   R Klein, 'Accountability in the Health Service' (1974) *Political Quarterly*.

It has been cogently argued that as a concept, choice is generic; a fertile notion which can encompass a *whole bundle of fundamental human rights* which are recognised as giving meaning to the very nature of the human endeavour towards self-fulfilment. Central to human rights is autonomy or freedom of expression. The Universal Declaration of Human rights states that everyone has the right to freedom of thought, conscience and to freedom of opinion and expression[14] and the European Convention on Human Rights and Fundamental Freedoms reflects these declarations.[15] Choice carries with it all the connotations of autonomy and freedom of expression and is thus endemic to the human condition. It is because of this and its multi-layered properties that some aspects of choice have found favour and expression, but only in a narrow individualist sense, in the ideology of the political right and current public sector reforms.[16]

But if choice is generic, freedom to choose logically extends beyond any restricted, individualist expression in economic markets into the political and social arena. The concept of choice therefore fuses the division of functions *generally* attributed to the market and to the field of politics. After all, individuals are social agents who must make their choices in the social arena where such choices are mutually affective and where collective responsibilities and entitlements necessarily operate. Autonomy is expressed through choice at different levels and in a number of different settings. This being the case, choice clearly encapsulates channels for both a *collegiate* as well as *individual* expression.

It is here where the constitutional dimension becomes apparent. A constitution is in essence a collective set of principles which gives credence to the fact that at the most fundamental level there are certain conditions which need to prevail and be actively pursued in order to allow citizens freedom of expression and further their well being. The constitution and the process of constitutional discussion should be a stabilising force, constitutional law being the basis around which all other law, regulation and social policy revolve. The role of a constitution is thus to secure and guarantee human rights and to reinforce the principles for debate about the exercise of choice in the political and social field. It provides a stable backdrop against which to ensure the provision of sufficient opportunity and means for all. A bedrock of opportunities must be provided which individuals may

---

14   See Articles 18 and 19.

15   Articles 9 and 10.

16   N Lewis, *Choice and the Legal Order* (Butterworths, 1996).

exercise or not according to their preferences. On a practical level this requires governance.

Whereas the role of the constitution is to guarantee immutable core values, the function of government, which is naturally subordinate to the constitution, is to facilitate discussion of remaining optional areas. This is because the government and those emanations which exercise functions on behalf of it, are constitutional agents with constitutional duties and consequently must act in accordance with constitutional principles. The actual *structures* for choice are therefore a matter for political debate and whilst they should strive to be optimal, no particular institutional arrangement or method of operation is prescribed. Once the constitution is accepted as the base from which everything else flows, there is no longer any need to think in terms of public and private. Political discussion will consider the extent and form of choice and the levels at which these might most effectively occur, as this may be different for different policy areas. The art of governance requires that there is sensitivity to the needs of various and different constituencies of interest. This means more than a superficial and cursory glance at accountability and participation in public decision-making, but the maximum impact possible of any particular voice. For freedom and self-fulfilment to be properly satisfied, choice needs to be promoted at the lowest level that it can occur most effectively. Thus the aim of collective choice is to facilitate as far as possible individual choice.[17] This, in effect, is the logical extension of the principle of subsidiarity.

Choice, of course, also implies a diversity of options from which to choose. Where limited resources constrain options, accountability requires that all citizens have an opportunity to have a say in choices about those limitations, or at the very least have limitations and the reasons for them made explicit. The central prerequisite for genuine choice and accountability is inevitably openness. The very right to seek, receive and impart information and ideas is deemed by the Universal Declaration of Human Rights to be central to freedom of expression. Since the values that underlie the provision of information influence awareness of alternatives and priorities, issues may too readily be prevented from being the subject of proper debate and thus reduce capacity for reasoned choices to be made about priorities and resource use. A commitment to transparency is of prime importance so that any tendency that there might be to control or distort information might be counteracted. The use of information either in isolation of other factors or ignorance of the perspective from which it has been

---

17   For a cogent account of this thesis see N Lewis, *ibid.*

generated can lead to a false impression of potential options and possible objectives. Unarticulated values not only shape priorities but influence the perceptions of problems and the feasibility of solutions. Consequent choices whether collective or individual will be exercised in a powerless vacuum and are likely to be ill-founded.

Furthermore, a commitment to openness means that more than a basic provision for access to information is needed. An effective exercise of choice entails the provision of both *relevant* and *adequate* information. To be successful openness requires the devising of mechanisms for the actual *generation* of information and its utilisation, in order to widen policy options. The same commitment also implies an obligation on the part of decision-makers to give explanations and justifications for their activities. The articulation of reasons for action or inaction is beneficial to choice and accountability in several ways. It not only assists the development of standards and principles, but encourages more care and deliberation on the purposes of action and provides a basis for criticism and facilitates challenge to decisions which appear arbitrary.[18]

THE ROLE OF LAW IN THE EXERCISE OF CHOICE

There is little established law or direct legislation governing the exercise of power about the allocation of resources in the National Health Service (NHS).[19] In fact, with a few notable exceptions, it is only recently that lawyers have begun to pay attention to the contribution that law can make to policy choices in the United Kingdom. This is perhaps surprising as one of the key functions of law in any society is to provide a framework for the conduct of public affairs. Law is traditionally one of the major means by which institutions such as those which provide health care, education or welfare benefits are established, defined and structured.[20] As statutory frameworks are, for the most part, enabling legislation which merely outline policy objectives and leave the detail of service provision to the exercise of delegated discretionary powers, law is also continually being made and interpreted within public institutions as policy choices are taken and put into practice.

---

18 D Galligan, 'Judicial Review and the Textbook Writers' (1992) *Oxford Journal of Legal Studies* Vol 2.

19 A Parkin, 'Allocating Health Care Resources in an Imperfect World (1995) MLR Vol 58.

20 R Cotterall and B Bercusson, 'Law Democracy and Social Justice' (1988) *Journal of Law and Society*.

Law clearly has both constraining and facilitative qualities and is instrumental in achieving public ends through the shaping of social processes. But it should also be emphasised that law is more than an instrument in that, it is a means of promoting choice and ensuring accountability in public decision-making; those principles which are the cornerstone of human rights and constitutional protections. Although discretionary powers are a necessary feature of modern government, enabling public bodies to cope with changing circumstances with a degree of flexibility, our concept of rights requires that such powers are neither abused nor exercised unfairly.

Procedures which facilitate choice and promote accountability help to ensure that arbitrary decisions are eliminated and that policy is made for reasons that are properly related to the objectives of the social enterprise. Thus, decisions are required to be made within a framework of principle rather than one of pragmatism. It has been widely recognised by constitutional commentators that procedures for choice and accountability through traditional democratic parliamentary processes, although supplemented and improved to some extent in recent years, fall far short of meeting modern demands for machinery that responds effectively to public policy needs. Yet our system is still in many ways attempting to come to terms with the failure of these traditional forms of law to deal with the current crises of legitimacy that have arisen in many of our public institutions and services.[21]

Where traditional means of securing fundamental ideals prove inadequate it follows that renewed consideration has to be given to other ways of perfecting arrangements for their realisation. In public institutions any fresh transfusion of means to re-vitalise those values and principles should seek to optimise opportunities for effective scrutiny and choice into processes for priority setting and resource allocation from those most affected.

This is of course easier said than done. Decision-making in the public arena has always been influenced by a perplexing heterogeneous mix of fiscal, managerial, professional and other public factors. Consequently, injecting effective choice and public accountability into decision-making processes is a no easy task. This is likely to be especially so in a highly specialised organisation such as the NHS, where choice and accountability have always been particularly complex and elusive concepts. Although the NHS is one of the most pervasive of all public services and a major contributor to decision-making which seemingly touches everyone at some time in

---

21   Parkin, *op cit* note 19.

their lives, health policy is an area to which public lawyers are just awakening.[22] Analysis by lawyers has been mainly peripheral; the interrelationship between law and health has been renowned mostly for consideration of liability for personal injury, medico-ethical issues and forensic matters. Health law has only occasionally focused on the justifications for the provision and allocation of services under the public financing and regulation of the system. These areas have, for the most part, been dominated by economic and management theory analysts.

One of the most comprehensive and rational considerations of the role of law was advocated by Karl Llewellyn.[23] He argued that in order for any group or institution, regardless of its size, to sustain stability and cohesiveness and thus function effectively a series of socially necessary tasks have to be performed. Like choice these fundamental jobs do not indicate the adoption of any *specific* organisational or procedural arrangements as these will be shaped by the context within which they are to operate, but they do provide a kind of blueprint for collective activity.

There are four main *interlinked* activities which Llewellyn dubbed the law-jobs, which can shape and contour the exercise of public power within the framework of modern policy making.[24] With specific reference to the health care field these are:

- The allocation of decision-making authority. The question of who is competent and who should have the power to make choices and decisions is crucial to the legitimacy and effectiveness of an organisation. It involves the structural and administrative framework within which the other tasks are carried out. This law-job is one which therefore brings into focus the exercise and control of delegated and discretionary powers and within the health service raises questions of the balance of authority and responsibility for the utilisation of resources between management, clinicians and of course the public.

- Choosing goals and objectives, the setting of priorities and development of policy. Within health care disparities in the allocation of resources can lead to injustice and unequal opportunity in the receipt of care. This means that health policy needs to be continually reassessed as information becomes available

---

22 Parkin, *op cit* R James and D Longley, 'Judicial Review and Choices: *ex parte* B' (1995) PL 367, C Newdick, 1 *Medical Law Review* (1993) 53.

23 K Llewellyn, 'The Normative, the Legal and the Law Jobs' (1940) *Yale Law Journal* 49.

24 N Lewis, 'Towards a Sociology of Lawyering in Public Administration' (1981) *Northern Ireland Legal Quarterly* and D Longley *Public Law and Health Service Accountability* (Open University Press, 1993).

about the possibilities for improving overall health status, prophylactic measures and the facilities for care. These are essentially political choices and the means for making them need to be embodied in the structure of the system to ensure legitimacy.

- The implementation of policy and monitoring of activity to ensure that chosen objectives are achieved. Monitoring is increasingly significant and evident in the processes of modern public management and is especially apparent in recent developments within health services. Monitoring may be either internal or external and is necessary for both the recognition and avoidance of disputes.

- The resolution of disputes. This concerns the redress of all grievances relating to the system; matters which are crucial to questions of legitimacy and accountability. Although individually a dispute or complaint may not pose any threat to the stability and cohesion of a society or organisation, accumulatively they may come to endanger the established order. Furthermore grievance resolution can provide additional information and feedback of the system in operation and an effective channel of accountability.

In short, the law-jobs provide the conditions for genuine accountability of collective decisions or choices through outlining the legitimate pattern of authority, the provision of information, and the machinery for policy making and the resolution of conflict. They thus help create a capacity for the public to obtain a clearer, wider and undistorted view of the operation and effectiveness of an organisation. Law is in effect perceived as a political resource that can be used to redesign social institutions to assist the co-ordination of action within and upon the system.

Thus, as management of public service rapidly changes and the legitimacy of policy choices becomes increasingly problematic, lawyers have a fundamental role to play in the analysis and development of the operation of our institutions. Since these matters concern the sharing of public power amongst government in its broadest sense[25] and other strategic groups, they should be of considerable importance to public lawyers, posing for them the questions that need to be asked before possible solutions can be considered. How are decisions made? By whom? On what criteria? How are differences of influence to be negotiated and resolved? Are the ways and means to achieve constitutional objectives effective?

---

25   'Less government but not less governance' as Osborne and Gaebler have put it. *Op cit.*

The main pursuit for lawyers is to actively assist in the attainment of substantive principles and the development of procedures which seek to infuse fundamental values of choice and accountability into our public, institutional structures. Through properly responsive processes of law a clearer picture can emerge, defects can be made apparent and the changing patterns of alliances can be highlighted. In this way an opportunity can be provided for different views and interests to be brought to bear on practice and ultimately act as a motor for change.

THE PLACE OF EFFICIENCY

Latterly, the emphasis of the management of public services and its correlation with markets has been on efficiency, particularly economic efficiency. Unfortunately this pursuit of efficiency seems to have given rise to a misconception in the public management field that the requirements of wider, public input and accountability are either irrelevant to or at least a constraint on its attainment.[26] Contrary to this it can be argued that accountability is closely linked to efficiency and to effectiveness which is sometimes subsumed within the former. Both efficiency and effectiveness are without doubt essential concerns in any enterprise, but they are complex and ambiguous concepts whose determination is particularly problematic within the health sector.

Put simply, effectiveness is an evaluative measure which is concerned with the attainment of intended objectives and the quality of outcomes, it is quite different in nature from efficiency. Efficiency concerns the optimum use of resources and the maximisation of output in relation to cost. Efficiency cannot be properly judged unless the criteria for effectiveness and quality are known. Hence, efficiency should be subordinate to effectiveness. Legitimacy of choice, or accountability for decisions taken, is logically an indispensable pre-condition for the advancement of both.[27]

The foregoing argument is not intended to deny that efficiency, effectiveness and quality may frequently be competing goals between which trade-offs have to be made. But freedom to choose requires that such trade-offs be made explicit. Any tendency to conflate all three factors into a concern for budgetary matters, particularly in an area

---

26 Ranson and Stewart, 'Citizenship and Government, the challenge for management in the public domain' (1989) *Political Studies*.

27 P Birkinshaw, I Harden and N Lewis, *Government by Moonlight; the hybrid parts of the state* (London: Unwin Hyman, 1990).

such as health care where uncertain and changing factors may critically affect the public interest, means that policy is not the consequence of the open and reasoned decision-making that choice and accountability dictate should be the case.

The process of public sector reform is unlikely to be regarded as legitimate and successful if guided only by instrumental rather than evaluative considerations. The justification for the market is not simply efficiency, since efficiency is a means not an end, justification lies in facilitating choice and delivery of those choices. Truly effective and hence efficient action by any organisation requires a capacity to learn through its arrangements for the setting and revising of objectives and policies and the monitoring of performance. Such arrangements constitute its procedures for justifying and testing the legitimacy of its decisions and conduct; the examination of which assists the learning process by the recognition of any real and potential differences in the perception of objectives and of competing priorities throughout an institutions networks and initiatives.

If the foregoing, briefly described concept of law and its duties is applied to the provision of health care it can be seen that any discussion of the socio-economic problems of health services and reform needs to be supported and broadened by examination of the organisation's constitutional expectations and the arrangements which underpin them. This necessitates a close look at how provisions for choice and user input are operating throughout the system. It is against this background that the constitutional arrangements and the health service reforms of New Zealand, Canada and the United Kingdom are examined.

CONSTITUTIONAL BACKGROUNDS

A number of common and interrelated factors have influenced reform in Canada, New Zealand and the United kingdom. But there are also pertinent considerations particular to one or another of the countries. Canada is a federal country, whilst New Zealand and the United Kingdom are for the most part unitary states. Thus, some activities of the national governments of the latter two countries are dealt with by the Canadian provincial governments. Whilst all three countries have 'Westminster' type parliamentary systems, differences amongst them – for example New Zealand has a single legislative chamber – have an impact on the ease with which reforms can be brought about and therefore on the nature of the reforms themselves.

Canada

The political and legal traditions of Canada owe much to those of the UK in that a fundamental principle of the Canadian constitution is parliamentary supremacy and there has been provision for judicial review since long before the federation came into being in 1867. In 1982 Canada entered a new phase in the evolution of its constitution when the Constitution Act came in to force and marked the final stage in the nation's move towards a fully independent status.[28] Of even more significance was the incorporation, by the 1982 Act, into the Canadian constitutional framework, of the *Canadian Charter of Rights and Freedoms.*

The Charter sets out a number of guaranteed rights and freedoms which are part of the supreme law of Canada. Any law or action taken by government which violates these fundamental rights and freedoms must be declared unconstitutional by the courts, unless they come within s 1. Section 1 is to some extent unusual in a national constitution in that it explicitly permits a certain derogation from the guarantee of fundamental rights. It allows for the possibility that circumstances might arise where such rights may nevertheless be limited or curtailed, as long as the limits put upon them by law are considered reasonable and can be justified.[29] Under the Charter the courts have been given:

> the task of developing some kind of balance between fundamental rights of citizens on the one hand, and the right and obligation of democratically elected governments to govern on the other hand.[30]

The onus of justification rests on governments, is rigorous and is not easily met. More unusually, the Canadian Charter contains what has come to be known as the 'notwithstanding clause'. Under s 33 the legislature may, by express declaration, provide that its legislation is to be operative even though it violates certain rights guaranteed under the Charter. This represents the ultimate compromise in the preservation of the traditional doctrine of parliamentary sovereignty within the modern context of judicial review, as it allows governments to have the final word in limited circumstances.[31] The provision

---

28 B Wilson, *The Making of a Constitution; approaches to judicial interpretation* [1988] Public Law 370.

29 The US Constitution has no comparable provision, but the Universal Declaration of Human Rights and the International Covenant on Civil and Political Rights and the European Convention all contain articles expressly authorising limits to be put on guaranteed rights.

30 Wilson, *op cit* p 371.

31 The Charter was painstaking negotiated as it was seen by many as irreconcilable with the concept of legislative supremacy. These arguments are not unfamiliar in the UK. See B L Strayer *Life under the Canadian Charter; adjusting the balance between legislatures and courts* [1988] PL 347.

permits override of the Charter for a period of five years only and has been invoked only rarely, as it would in all likelihood spell political suicide for any government that attempted it.

Canada, like New Zealand and the UK has been subject to public sector reform, though perhaps not to the same extent. In December 1989 the government announced a process of reform and renewal of the federal public service. This initiative, known as Public Service 2000 was 'the policy of the Government of Canada concerning the measures necessary to safeguard and promote efficiency and professionalism of the Public Service in order that it may serve Canadians effectively in the 21st century'.[32] Measures taken included a reduction of administrative controls to give deputy ministers greater freedom to manage their departments and clearer accountability for results; simplification and clarification of the roles of central agencies and administrative control throughout government and innovative ways to encourage efficiency and improve programme delivery. There was also increased emphasis on openness and consultation.

Canada has created some new organisational forms designed to improve service delivery and cost effectiveness, but these have tended not to have gone as far in terms of commercialisation and separation of operation from policy, as has been the case in the UK and particularly New Zealand. Further, there appears to have been neither interest in nor active support at the political level for the initiative as a whole, in spite of the passage of a Public Sector Reform Act in 1992. This may be significant in that in Canada a key theme was improving service to the public rather than the more strategic approach to public management and public service reform taken in the other two countries. The latter concentrated more on the question of the affordability of government services.[33]

New Zealand

In constitutional terms, New Zealand is similar to the UK from which it derived many if its traditions and structures. Possibly because of this British inheritance a fault of New Zealand's constitutional system is that it is possible to make changes rapidly with insufficient public consultation. A key feature is a concentration of power in central government particularly the executive arm; the cabinet and the public services sector. Although in recent years some innovative changes have

---

32 *Canada's Public Service Reform, and Lessons Learned from Selected Jurisdictions* (Report of the Auditor General, 1993).

33 *ibid* p 178.

been made these have tended not to alter significantly the basic structure.

There is no single, formal document or statement of what constitutes the New Zealand constitution. Rather, the constitution is a series of concepts that have evolved over time and which comprise both those laws which define the structure and principles of government and those laws, customs and conventions defining the composition and powers of agencies of state and their relationships with citizens. Of key significance is the Constitution Act (1986) which brings together certain provisions of constitutional significance and defines the separation of powers and the Bill of Rights Act (1990) which affirms, protects and promotes human rights and fundamental freedoms in New Zealand. It also affirms New Zealand's commitment to the International Covenant on Civil and Political Rights (1978). Unlike the Canadian Charter, the Constitution Act and the Bill of Rights Act are not entrenched and have the status of ordinary legislation.[34] In other words neither will override other primary legislation and are capable of being amended or repealed,[35] but any inconsistency must be drawn to the notice of Parliament. The Bill of Rights is clearly intended to provide a restraint on the power of the executive and to bring the values expressed in it to bear on the legislative and administrative processes.[36]

The legitimacy of decision-making and its outcomes is also enhanced by the Official Information Act (1982) which expresses the principle of:

increasing progressively the availability of official information to the people of New Zealand in order

(i) to enable their more effective participation in the making and administration of laws and policies; and

(ii) to promote the accountability of Ministers of the Crown and officials.[37]

New Zealand governments have traditionally taken a very active role in economic development. Like the UK the highly centralised nature of power in New Zealand was reflected in the public services. The state has provided health, education and welfare services, but it has also

---

34 The wording of the Act, for the most part, is taken directly from the Canadian Charter of Rights and Freedoms.

35 See generally G Palmer, *New Zealand's Constitution in Crisis* (1992). Despite not being entrenched Palmer points to the potential importance of the Bill of Rights Act and the use already made of it.

36 See J McClean, P Rishworth and M Taggart, 'The Impact of the New Zealand Bill of Rights on Administrative Law' [1992] *Administrative Law* 62.

37 Section 4(a) Official Information Act (1982).

developed active interests in such diverse areas as shipping, roads, banking, the tourist and insurance industries, as well as in communications and broadcasting. Many of the changes that have occurred in the management of public services in New Zealand mirror those taking place in the UK, but in contrast to the UK, New Zealand's reforms have been accompanied by legislation, improved deliberative powers for Parliament and an effective Ombudsman who is also Official Information Commissioner.[38]

Since 1984 there has been a strong commitment to the greater use of market mechanisms and a corresponding distrust of administrative solutions to problems.[39] Changes in economic theory and practice have been reflected in similar changes to the public sector. There has inevitably been a shift away from a highly centralised and uniform public sector towards a culture that has focused on the distinctive role of particular agencies and the introduction of incentives and accountabilities to improve management performance.

The greatest change has been the corporatisation of some government functions in that many 'commercial' activities of government departments have been removed from the core public service and set up as limited liability companies, termed State Owned Enterprises (SOE). All shares in SOEs are held by the Crown and there are intensive arrangements for monitoring performance. With the establishment of SOEs the remaining core public service included a mix of policy, regulatory and operational functions which covers the supply of health, education and social services amongst others. These areas now come under the State Sector Act (1988), the basic thrust of which was to redefine the relationship between Ministers and chief executives and ensure that the latter be held accountable. However, under the Act chief executives have very substantial freedom to decide how to deliver the services for which they are responsible.

The United Kingdom

It is well known that the UK has no written constitution. This gives rise to a number of difficulties, but it does not mean of course that there is no constitution. Although first principles might be difficult to identify in a British setting, they do exist. Embedded in our system are a number of sentiments and understandings of a cultural nature which belong to the familiar collection of human rights and which are upheld

---

38   N Lewis, *The Next Steps Initiative* (Report to the Leverhulme Foundation, 1993).

39   *New Zealand Public Sector Reform* (State Service Commission, 1993).

by our common law.[40] In other words there are certain broad propositions which have arisen from our history, culture and political obligations which are approved of widely if not generally. But precisely because they are unwritten and unclear these sentiments and understandings can be treated in a more cavalier manner than would be the case if they were part of a coherent constitution which actually articulated fundamental values.[41] The UK also possesses a separate procedure for the pursuit of public law rights through an uncodified system of judicial review which has an extremely long pedigree and which underpins distinct expectations of fairness in the public sphere.

However, unfortunately in the UK there has been no *serious* commitment to open government and freedom of information legislation, which lies at the heart of a commitment to freedom of expression and choice, increasingly evident in other developed democracies. This has had a profound effect on citizen access to decision-making.

In the UK the origins of NPM arguably date from 1982 and the Financial Management Initiative (FMI) which sought to tighten accountability for public sector expenditure and was extended to the health service under the title of the Resource Management Initiative. Since 1988 the perceived weaknesses of FMI have led to a more thorough re-organisation of government departments, beginning with the Next Steps programme. Through Next Steps there has been a devolution of government department functions to a wide variety of agencies, ostensibly outside direct ministerial control. This has been supplemented by privatisation of some civil service tasks and, latterly, the adoption of market testing and contracting out strategies.[42]

Hence each country has been instituting public sector reforms against different constitutional backgrounds, albeit all have had a strong British pedigree. In all three countries health services reforms have not taken quite the same form as in other public sector areas, but they have nevertheless been considerably influenced by the general trends of NPM. Given these developments the question Is whether there is anything that can be learned, each from the other, so as to advance the central thesis of choice? It is to this issue that the next three chapters now turn.

---

40 This increasingly also appears to be the case with the European Convention on Human Rights to which the UK was one of the original signatories, but which has never been incorporated directly into our domestic law.

41 N Lewis and D Longley, *Ethics in Public Service* [1994] PL 596.

42 See in particular the De-regulation and Contracting Out Act (1994)

CHAPTER 2

CANADIAN HEALTH SERVICES

INTRODUCTION

The provision of health care in Canada has changed fundamentally in the last 20 years or so. These changes are encompassed by the constitutional division of powers which exists between federal and provincial levels of government. Whilst the delivery of services is the responsibility of the Canadian provinces, both federal and provincial legislation has a significant role in setting out the scope of health care through the system of funding, the allocation of resources and the definition of the services to be provided.

Discussion of health services in Canada is complicated by the fact that there is really no one system, but rather 12 distinct systems organised by the 10 provinces and two territories. Despite the multiplicity of systems however, there are a number of shared basic features which have arisen from the agreements made between the provinces, territories and the federal government as regards funding and provision. For the most part what follows in this chapter refers to the provinces of Nova Scotia particularly, Alberta and British Colombia which all differ from each other not only in demographic terms but in prosperity as well.

Initially health care in Canada was regarded as a matter of concern for the family, a variety of volunteer and charitable organisations and the market. There was no specific mention of health care in Canada's founding document, the Constitution Act (1897). Those health care issues that arose within constitutional litigation were usually concerned with jurisdictional disputes between the different levels of government about responsibility for the prevention of the spread of disease.[1] From the 1930s an increasing number of commercial insurance companies introduced medical policies and in some provinces doctors banded together to develop their own competing profession controlled prepayment plans. In 1943 the Canadian Medical Association formally approved the idea of a national health insurance plan although it did not really envisage any role for government, other than providing subsidies for those who could not afford to pay their

---

1   H Lessard, 'The Construction of Health Care and the Ideology of the Private in Canadian Constitutional Law' (1993) *Annals of Health Law* Vol 2:121.

own premiums. Gradually however a combination of social, political and economic factors, pressure from a variety of groups concerned with welfare and social reform, and the breakdown of a series of *ad hoc* reforms led to a more comprehensive public response to health care issues.[2] A number of provinces introduced publicly funded hospital care insurance schemes, and then in 1961 a joint agreement between federal and provincial governments led to the development of a national hospital insurance scheme. In 1964 the Royal Commission on Health Services recommended that provincial governments should take over the administration of health insurance plans from the private sector and that the plans be fully and universally subsidised by federal and provincial governments rather than paid for by individual subscription.

These recommendations were implemented in the Medical Care Act (1966) to form a national Medicare system in which all provinces and territories eventually participated.[3] In principle, by the early 1970s the Medical Care Act had established a system of free and universal health care throughout Canada. However in the next 10 years the imposition of user fees by hospitals and extra billing by doctors became widespread. These practices were seen to undermine the principle that all Canadians should have access to health care irrespective of their individual ability to pay. Consequently in 1984 the federal government enacted the Canada Health Act which now sets out the terms and conditions for the national Medicare programme.

The Act's primary objective is stated to be the protection, promotion and restoration of the physical and mental well-being of Canadians and the facilitation of reasonable access to health services without financial or other barriers.[4] Medicare is intended to be an open-ended scheme with regard to reimbursement of service costs. There is no *individual* limit on reimbursement no matter how often the person falls ill or how expensive the treatment. The Act does not prohibit *per se* the provision of private health care services. Rather, under threat of federal funds being withdrawn it prevents provinces and territories, from allowing providers to bill patients directly for amounts over and above that received for medically necessary services under provincial health insurance plans. Providers are able to opt out altogether from provincial health insurance plans and charge patients directly for the

---

2   J P Dickin McGinnis, 'Whose Responsibility? Public Health in Canada 1919-1945' (1981) in *Doctors, Patients and Society* (M Staum and D Larsen Eds, Wilfred Laurier University Press).

3   It was not until 1972 that all provinces and territories met with requirements of the underlying legislation. M G Taylor, *Health insurance and Canadian Public Policy* (McGill-Queens University Press, 1978).

4   The Canada Health Act, SC (1984) Chapter 6 s 3.

full cost of services. In this case patients will also be ineligible for reimbursement from provincial insurance.

The finance which comes from both federal and provincial levels of government to meet the objectives of the Canada Health Act accounts for 75% of Canadian health expenditure. The remaining 25% is borne by individuals either directly or through supplementary insurance plans. Expenses for drugs, optical and medical devices and dental care, all of which are excluded from most provincial and territorial health insurance plans, frequently come from employers providing group cover. The health care insurance plans run by provincial governments charge residents a health care insurance premium and must operate on a non-profit basis. However, there is no single health tax in Canada as the system is financed through income, sales and business tax and through other schemes devised by provinces to raise revenue. Federal government transfers funds to provinces in respect of services which are defined in the Act as 'medically necessary' for the purpose of maintaining health, preventing disease, or diagnosing or treating an injury, illness or disability.'[5]

To qualify for the full, federal contribution, insurance schemes devised by provinces have to satisfy the five basic principles which are set out in the Act. Plans must be administered publicly, must be comprehensive, universal, portable and provide accessibility.[6] Furthermore extra billing and user fees other than for accommodation or meals provided to in-patients who need constant care and are permanently hospitalised or resident in some other institution is not permitted.[7] If any of these principles or conditions are not met, the federal government contribution may be reduced or withheld. Thus, violation of the principles of the Act, though not strictly speaking illegal, is made financially unattractive. Sanctions for non-compliance hit provinces where it is most likely to have an effect, that is 'in the pocket', and encourages medical activity to be monitored. In effect, the Canada Health Act does not regulate health care providers directly, but simply sets out the terms on which federal cash transfers will be made.

In accordance with the Act, provincial regulation lists those medically necessary treatments and procedures that will be reimbursed by the provincial government. However, although these provisions influence accessibility and availability in general terms, procedures that are deemed necessary by the medical profession and patient are neither prohibited nor restricted.

---

5   *ibid* s 2.

6   *ibid* ss 7-12.

7   *ibid* ss 18-21.

Aside from the statutory conditions set out in the Canada Health Act, the *Canadian Charter of Rights and Freedoms* also arguably supports the provision of health care. Unlike the United Kingdom (UK) and New Zealand, Canada has a written constitution. The *Canadian Charter of Rights and Freedoms* was constitutionally entrenched in 1982 as part 1 of the Constitution Act. The Charter applies to all governments – federal, provincial and territorial – and protects those 'basic rights and freedoms essential to maintaining a free and democratic society and a united country'. Since the entrenchment of the Charter a wide range of social issues including health care have been increasingly discussed in terms of rights. Section seven of the Charter states:

> Everyone has the right to life, liberty and security of the person and the right not to be deprived thereof except in accordance with the principles of fundamental justice.

It can be claimed credibly that s 7 guarantees a constitutional right to health care. In practical terms a right to life and security is meaningless without access to health care both in a preventative and treatment sense. This argument has been endorsed by the Law Reform Commission in Canada which has suggested that the right to security of person means not only the protection of physical integrity but the provision of what is necessary to support it.[8]

With the advent of the Charter, the Canada Health Act and the Medicare system both Canadian citizens and governments have come to regard free and universal health care as a basic right of citizenship.[9] In *Stoffman v Vancouver General Hospital* (1990) it was stated that 'government has recognised for some time that access to basic health care is something no sophisticated society can legitimately deny any of its members'.[10] Similarly Jackman points out that an interpretation of s 7 that includes a right to health care reflects the broader social context within which the Charter was adopted and the background against which the Supreme Court has agreed the Charter must be understood.[11] It is also consistent with Canada's extensive commitments to international human rights in the area of social and economic rights, including health.[12]

Weller has described Canadian health care provision as a 'subsidised entrepreneurial model 'rather than a socialised system of

---

8   M Jackman, *The Regulation of Private Health Care in Canada under the Canada Health Act and the Canadian Charter* (1994) Constitutional Forum pp 54-60.

9   M Begin, *Medicare, Canada's Right to Health* (Montreal, Optimum Publishing, 1988).

10   Mrs Justice Wilson (1990) 3 RSC 483:544.

11   M Jackman, 'The Protection of Welfare Rights under the Charter' (1988) 20 *Ottawa L Review* 257.

12   *ibid* and see the Universal Declaration of Human Rights, Article 25 and the International Covenant on Economic Social and Cultural Rights, Ariclet 12 which are endorsed by Canada.

medicine'.[13] Doctors in Canada are not salaried, but paid on a fee-for-service basis. This has meant that they have held a strong negotiating position with provincial governments with regard to fee schedules and carry considerable weight in defining basic health care and what is regarded as medically necessary. The emphasis through the influence of the medical profession has tended to favour curative rather than preventative measures and an imbalance between primary and acute sectors of care. This is a pattern not unfamiliar elsewhere and one that has certainly been reflected in the provision of the UK and New Zealand health services.

The determination of what actually constitutes insured health services has always been a matter of some controversy between federal and provincial governments in Canada and is a significant factor in the debates that Canadians have been having recently about the implications of current reforms in terms of privatisation of the health system. The problem arises from the interpretation of the term 'medically necessary or required' used to describe insured health services in federal legislation. The Canada Health Act defines insured health services as hospital services, physician services and surgical-dental services. Hospital services are defined quite specifically but those of physicians and surgical-dental services are not. Provinces are able to determine what services fall within the ambit of medically required and are therefore 'insured health services' giving rise to reimbursement. The problem is that provinces have failed to define or set out the criteria on which 'medically required' is to be established. Instead medical procedures are simply listed in regulation which may be changed administratively. Consequently a provincial government may remove a service from the list of insured health services, the service then loses its character of being medically required. In the recent atmosphere of fiscal constraint a number of previously available, albeit as yet minor, procedures have been removed from insured services.[14] This inevitably puts pressure on the patient's pocket either directly or through increased private or employer premiums which might have to be paid to cover services not insured publicly.

As with other countries Canada has been experiencing 'medical inflation' and potentially unlimited increases in expenditure associated with epidemiological changes and technological advances. As a result federal government has adopted a policy to limit progressively its

---

13 G R Weller, 'Pressure Group Politics to Medical Industrial Complex. The Development of Approaches to the Politics of Health Care' (1980) in *Perspectives on Canadian Health and Social Services Policy: History and Emerging Trends* (C Meilecke and J Storch Eds).

14 For example in Alberta wart removal, eye examination and general anaesthetic for some dental surgery are no longer covered by the provincial health plan.

financial contributions to health care which has put considerable pressure on provincial and territorial health services. The poorer provinces such as Nova Scotia which have few if any resources to replace the federal shortfall, have had to resort to cutting services and freezing salaries. The wealthier provinces such as Alberta and British Columbia have only been able to maintain present services by cutting expenditure on other public service areas or by running high deficits.[15]

As a consequence heath care systems across Canada have been under pressure to develop new strategies which restructure, rationalise and seek to improve efficiency. Whilst these strategies for health reform differ to some extent in each province in respect of detail, and are at different stages of implementation, a number of factors are discernible as common to all. Beside a continued commitment to principles of the Canada Health Act and a desire to ensure a more cost effective system there is a general recognition of the need to provide much better integrated services. Developments are generally characterised by a shift from institutional to community based provision and a re-alignment of responsibility for planning and delivery. There is also a clear commitment to the consideration of health matters in all aspects of public policy and an emphasis on health promotion.

There are also a number of conceptual changes which have embraced for the most part a more dynamic and consultative approach to reform and which highlight the role of the citizen or consumer as an active partner in the development of community networks of health care services.

GENERAL HEALTH CARE RE-ORGANISATION IN CANADA

Reform and change are thus the order of the day for health care in Canada. Virtually every jurisdiction has undertaken a major review either by the establishment of a Royal Commission or a special task force to look at health care administration and costs.[16] As might be expected, each of these reports reached very similar conclusions from their investigations and analysis of the evidence submitted to them.

The major recommendations of these reviews can briefly be listed under five main headings:

---

15 D Ray, J Williams and B Dickens, *Bioethics in Canada* (Prentice Hall, 1994) Chapter 4.

16 For example *Towards a New Strategy* (Report of the Nova Scotia Royal Commission on Health Care, December 1989) and *Closer to Home* (Report of the British Colombia Royal Commission on Health Care, 1991).

- *Financial resources* – shifting resources from acute care hospital services towards less expensive alternative ways of delivery such as home and community care and health promotion;

- *Human resources* – monitoring the number and practices of physicians and enhancing the role of other health professionals;

- *Organisation* – the take over of planning, administration and management of health programmes by regional health bodies and the development of pilot projects to test different delivery approaches;

- *Management* – improved management, planning, monitoring and information support, including the active involvement of health professionals; and

- *Other issues or trends* – taking account of demographic problems and the use of technology.[17]

In response to these general recommendations there has been a variety of initiatives at both national and provincial levels. In 1991 provincial and territorial Ministers of Health stated their commitment to a renewed health partnership with federal government and the protection and maintenance of the Canadian health system. Key concepts of this commitment were the preservation of the principles of the Canada Health Act; assurances of adequate funding and effective management of the system. They also identified a number of strategies, national in scope, to strengthen partnerships and to improve the effectiveness of the health system.

These included the development of national health goals, support for research into innovative and cost effective ways to deliver health care, the development of quality assurance, co-ordination of the supply and distribution of human resources and collaboration on the assessment and procurement of new technologies. Announcements were also made about the adoption of a national strategy in relation to the payment, training and competency of physicians and consideration of ways to ensure adequate funding and control costs.

Whilst these moves were taking place at a national level major initiatives were also being undertaken within the provinces, particularly in terms of consideration of the re-allocation of resources, the restructuring of administration and delivery of health care and related services.

---

17 'Health Care Reform Across Canada' (*Provincial Health Council Report*, December 1992, Appendix 3).

Generally these reviews concluded that there was a lack of direction in health care, a lack of local influence on policy, complicated by a too heavily centralised bureaucracy and a lack of openness which reinforced inequities and stifled initiative and change. Further, there was a need for more flexible and more representative health systems.

All in all, there is now a wide range of health care initiatives at various stages of implementation across the Canadian nation. Major changes are occurring in most provinces and every aspect of health care seems likely to feel the effects.

NOVA SCOTIA

The province of Nova Scotia covers an area of 55,500 sq km and has a population of under one million. This comprises 3.3% of the total Canadian population at a density of 16 people per sq km. Unemployment is high, around 14-15% and the province has suffered negative economic growth, giving it one of the worst performing economies in the country. Consequently, the government has charged itself with finding new and creative ways to maintain and improve public services, whilst spending less money and making public services more adaptable, accountable and client centred. This approach has initiated 'management audits' – systematic and independent analysis of government departments, programmes, services and personnel.

Nova Scotia spends about 27 cents of every dollar on health care, which makes it amongst the highest per capita spenders in Canada as a proportion of Gross Domestic Product (GDP). Despite this Nova Scotians are amongst the least healthy Canadians, having a lower life expectancy than people in other provinces. A higher rate of heart disease, cancer and pulmonary disease and disability is also experienced. Shortly after the introduction of Medicare, as in other provinces, concerns began to be expressed about health care use and escalating costs. In 1972 the Nova Scotia Council of Health concluded that the publicly funded system could be improved and costs contained to a level that the province could afford. It recommended the exploration of new ideas and extensive restructuring.[18] More recently the Nova Scotia Legislative Select Committee on Health likewise concluded that the health of Nova Scotians could be improved and significant savings realised by devising a strategy for the delivery of health services designed to prevent disease and promote health. As a

---

18 *Health care in Nova Scotia; a New Direction for the Seventies* (Halifax, 1972).

means of helping curtail institutional expansion, the Committee called for the introduction of a co-ordinated home care scheme.[19] However the shift to community care was limited and remained unavailable to the vast majority of Nova Scotians. In addition only minimal amounts of funding went towards health prevention, promotion and public health programmes. As a result, the health care system was regarded as predominately institutionalised, fiscally disproportionate and clearly lacking the benefits of a long term comprehensive plan.[20]

The Nova Scotia Royal Commission was set up in 1987 to inquire into and make recommendations with respect to health care. The Commission's remit was to:

- examine the costs of the health delivery system and recommend efficiencies which could be adopted to reduce costs while maintaining the effectiveness of programmes without imposing hospital user fees or direct charges for physician services;

- examine rates of increase in the costs of health care, including hospital care, medical services insurance, ambulance services, community health and drug dependency programmes and where possible identify the reasons for such increases;

- examine duplication of services and recommend methods to improve efficiency;

- assess the physician manpower requirements of the province;

- assess administrative efficiencies of hospitals and make recommendations in respect of alternative practices which would permit optimum efficiency in the hospitals and hospital system of the province;

- assess the costs incurred by teaching hospitals in respect of their responsibilities to medical schools and students.

From the start, the Commission adopted a broad interpretation of its mandate. In view of the magnitude and complexity of the health care system it was clear that an inquiry based on a narrow perspective focusing on cost alone would not suffice. The Commission felt that the broad social and economic dimensions of health necessitated a comprehensive approach. The Commission divided its activities into three streams: public hearings; research and consultations. The Commissioners recognised the importance of placing their work within the context of current trends locally, provincially, nationally and

---

19 Report of the Nova Scotia Legislative Select Committee on Health (Halifax, 1984).
20 Liberal Health Policy (1993).

internationally and adopted a participatory approach throughout the three streams.

A call for submissions appeared in all provincial newspapers and more than 2,700 information packages about public hearings were sent to voluntary organisations, health care organisations, professional associations, business groups, unions, physicians, nurses and interested citizens across the province. Public hearings were held throughout Nova Scotia and a summary of submissions and transcripts of the hearings was published in 1988 entitled *Issues and Concerns*. The Commission then entered its research phase where research areas were divided into three broad categories: economic, epidemiological and demographic information; health services administration; and health policy and planning. In addition to in-house research undertaken by Royal Commission staff studies were carried out on the Commission's behalf by a considerable number of other institutions.[21]

Representatives from the health sector were invited to attend sessions at which issues and options raised by research were discussed. The reactions of the participants in these sessions formed a significant part of the next consultative phase. In this third phase the Commissioners invited health care experts to participate in their seminars, travelled to other provinces, the United States and Europe and attended a number of major health policy conferences. The three streams of the Commission's investigation were consolidated at a policy finalisation session when leaders of health policy analysis from across Canada and Europe met with the royal Commission, reviewed its findings and provided guidance on the formulation of the Royal Commissions final recommendations. The final report was published at the end of 1989.[22]

The Royal Commission embraced a philosophy that espoused the 'inherent value and worth of each individual' and its fundamental tenet was that 'every Nova Scotian is entitled to realise his or her full physical, mental and spiritual potential'. In order to assist each and every person to achieve a full and healthy life the Commission underlined that federal and provincial governments must remain committed to the principle of a universal health system that is publicly funded. All the recommendations of the Commission were directed at this emphasis on the individual as the underlying basis of a publicly funded system, from strategic planning to the provision of patient care services.

---

21 The research studies were published as supplemental volumes to the final report of the Royal Commission.

22 *Towards a new Strategy* (The Report of the Nova Scotia Royal Commission on Health Care, December 1989).

The recommendations were also founded on the five following guiding principles:

Health policies oriented to healthy outcomes

To achieve the ultimate goal of maintaining individual well being and advance the health of society as a whole in ways that extract the most out of available resources, the province needed to invest in information systems that measured the results of its health policies. The Commission maintained that expenditures on health care must not expand at the expense of other essential social programmes so that adopting a comprehensive approach to health policy should help foster a better balance between the demands of health and other policies which contribute to overall health status.

Collective action should be aimed at both personal lifestyle and environmental conditions over which individuals have little direct control but which are directly correlated. Within the health care system itself not only must greater emphasis be placed on health promotion and illness prevention, but delivery systems must be reorganised to place greater reliance on non-institutional and ambulatory models, where care could be shifted to home and community settings. Such a restructuring could only succeed if built on a better understanding of precisely what the system was achieving. A new health strategy would therefore require constant analysis of the determinants of health and of the health status of citizens as well as evaluations of the efficiency and effectiveness of health programmes. Current information systems relied extensively on mortality and institutional morbidity data which gave an insight only into death and illness. Data concerning public health needed to be collected to identify needs prior to medical or hospital services actually being required. The Commission concluded that the province could 'ill afford the cost of not obtaining the types of information appropriate for assessment, planning and decision-making'.

Participation of citizens

As the population at large shared responsibility for wise use of limited health resources, the best way to mobilise people to accept a sense of stewardship of the health system was to empower them to act on health issues both *individually* and *collectively*. This process begins with the dissemination of information on all aspects of health as a key factor in facilitating responsibility and choice. Individuals could become partners with professionals in both the planning of health care and treatment processes. Collective empowerment enables interested parties to become involved in deciding what kind of health system is required and which health technology is appropriate for their needs.

The Commission pointed out that broad based participation would only occur when planning and decision-making moved closer to the beneficiaries of health services. The principle of empowerment forms the basis of decentralised decision-making and the development of regional structures for the delivery of health care.

Decentralisation and regionalisation

Regionalisation involved the adaptation of a network of services to the needs of a region, and decentralisation entails delegation of responsibility and authority to regional bodies. Centralisation of these functions had inhibited meaningful participation and as a result the system needed to devolve to allow participation of citizens and health care providers in the planning and management of health resources. Government had to recognise that it could not deal directly with the many varied and peripheral decisions required within the system. Neither had it the necessary specific or local knowledge, nor the capacity for responding quickly enough to local needs to manage all aspects of health services. Decentralisation would put operating authority in local hands. The Commission maintained that all health programmes should be planned and managed by Regional Health Authorities, within clear guidelines established by the provincial government. Regional priorities would be decided through participatory processes taking into consideration the experiences needs and views of local communities, health care providers and agencies.

For the delegation of authority to succeed the system required competent managers with the appropriate skills for specific tasks, as well as public input. Everyone would need to be committed to these changes, which could be stimulated by government through openness and a willingness to act in a flexible and co-operative way.

Accountability

An emphasis on decentralisation and wide participation in planning and management necessitated a high degree of accountability of those to whom authority had been delegated. The primary mandate of government was the overall direction of the health system but planning must be undertaken in consultation with those who had professional and community interests. This province wide planning process should begin with health goals and measurable objectives as the basis for regional accountability, Consequently information must not only be applied for the purpose of central planning by government but must be available to the health constituency for use at regional planning level. Bringing information and monitoring into the public forum would thus make the system more accountable for its performance.

Accountability and co-ordination would be strengthened by also providing health care professionals with opportunities to participate in planning and management. Financial incentives should also be used to advance management practice and professional decision-making, with respect to the way in which health services were offered and used.

Matching resources to local health needs

A new health strategy would strengthen the relationship between available resources and the health needs of the population. Changes must therefore occur in the delivery of services, the deployment of health personnel, the use of technology and the allocation of capital and financial resources if the Nova Scotia health system is to be efficient and genuinely concerned with the effectiveness of its programmes.

Health services in Nova Scotia emphasised acute care with delivery located primarily in the institutional setting. The Commission proposed changes to adjust the balance between the treatment of illness and the other components of health care. They regarded the greatest potential for advances to be made in community based services. Accordingly, some small community hospitals could develop a larger role as community health centres. Such restructuring was necessary to promote services that embraced health promotion, long term care, rehabilitation and palliative care as well as the treatment of acute disease.

The Commission added that health needs, not the aspirations of professional groups must drive human resource planning in the health service and strike the best mix between physicians and other health professionals. Multi-professional health care delivery teams needed to be developed to provide adequate levels of service in the future.

It was also pointed out that as rapid advances have been made in technology unrealistic expectations of what the health system can achieve have arisen. But like other health care resources the use of technology should reflect population based regional needs, otherwise fiscal pressures would continue to be created. Whilst information on clinical assessment can be gleaned from other jurisdictions, economic and ethical aspects of new developments must reflect local values and costs. Established practices that are characterised as low cost and high volume needed to be assessed as much as new and emerging 'high tech' procedures and equipment.

The Commission concluded that the Nova Scotia health system was on the whole adequately funded, but financial resources needed to be redistributed more equitably and managed more effectively. The funding of the system had to be approached as one component of an integrated economic strategy, with health expenditure controlled and managed to promote other vital aspects of the economy.

In short, the Royal Commission proposed innovations in the administration of the health care system, incorporating the guiding principles of a health policy aimed at good health, participation, decentralisation and accountability. Key to these changes were calls for a comprehensive health policy, provincial health council, a Ministry of Health and the formation of regional health authorities. In terms of the delivery of health services the guiding principles were to be aimed at outcomes, participation and the matching of resources to needs.

The Royal Commission's report has been dealt with at some length not only because it is the founding document of health reform in Nova Scotia, but to highlight the very different approach taken by the province to that of the inquiry set up by the Thatcher government in the UK. The Canadians espoused openness, participation and a thoroughness lacking in its hasty British counterpart. To some extent this reflects the difference in constitutional background and political cultures of the two countries which will also be evident through the approach adopted to health reforms in Alberta and British Columbia.

The government of Nova Scotia indicated its general acceptance of the Commission's report early in 1990 and announced several initial measures based on its recommendations. The Minister of Health set up an implementation committee to develop the government's overall response and elaborate a new strategy for health. The Committee undertook a detailed analysis of the Royal Commission's recommendations and consulted internally and externally with interest groups and other government departments. The results were published in *Health Strategy for the Nineties: Managing Better Health* which indicated the direction the Nova Scotia government intended to pursue in reforming the provinces health system. The long-term strategy and the guiding principles of the Commission were specifically endorsed and its recommendations were for the most part accepted.

The precepts on which the new strategy was to be based included a comprehensive, integrated and co-ordinated system supported by the introduction of six new Regional Health Agencies, although decentralisation was examined at a later date; a Provincial Health Council to provide a forum for broad public participation; a reorganised Department of Health to be addressed as a first priority; and various inter-departmental mechanisms to facilitate co-ordination of health within wider government policies. The system was to aim to be community-based, flexible and responsive to user's needs, offering a full continuum of care, ranging from health promotion, disease prevention, treatment and referral services to rehabilitation. Within the continuum of care increased emphasis was to be placed on strengthening primary care services.

A number of task forces were also set up to address many of the recommendations, including task forces on nursing, primary health care, physician policy development and a Ministerial Working Group on mental health services. In 1992 the Department of Health published a Progress Report[23] on the implementation of the recommendations of the Royal Commission and the initiatives of the Departments health strategy for the nineties. The document purported to demonstrate that in one way or another some action had been taken on 90% of the recommendations of the Royal Commission, which had either been completed, were underway or were in the planning stage. All of the initiatives of the Department had been implemented, were under review or awaiting the reports of the task forces. Although as a result of this drive Nova Scotia was at the leading edge of health planning in Canada progress was not particularly speedy, but at least it was in motion.

Of fundamental interest here are those changes which are deemed to enhance choice in health care policy, in particular the establishment of Regional Health organisations and in particular the Provincial Health Council.

The Provincial Health Council

The Nova Scotia Provincial Health Council was established in 1990 and was the first health council of its kind to be established by legislation in Canada.[24] The Council, including the chairperson, is made up of 12 volunteers from across the province who advise the government and are appointed by the Minister of Health. Any Nova Scotian can apply for appointment to the Council. Following their appointment the Council set up an office and hired an executive director and four other support staff. The Council has been in full operation since the beginning of 1992 and has established a number of committees to work

---

23 Department of Health (October 1992).
24 An Act to Establish a Provincial Health Council (1990) Chapter 13.

on specific projects. The committees may include persons who are not members of the Council and the Council may also call on the services of Department of Health staff, on the approval of the Deputy Minister.

The Council reports, through the Minister of Health, to the provincial government which also approves its budget and provides its operating funds. It is responsible for:

- encouraging people to take part in health planning;

- ongoing public education on health and health care;

- advising the government on specific health issues;

- preparing an annual report on the Council's activities, and an audit or report card on progress towards improving the health and health care system for Nova Scotians.

The first thing the Council did was to lay the groundwork for one of its major responsibilities – working with Nova Scotians to reform the health care system. This included developing a definition of 'health', establishing province-wide health goals and producing an overall framework for a comprehensive health strategy.

Building on the work of the World Health Organisation (WHO), in 1991 the Council adopted the following definition of health:

Health, for Nova Scotians, is a capacity, as individuals and as members of groups and communities, to function optimally and to improve their social and physical environment to achieve well-being.

Put more simply ...

Health is the capacity to function optimally and to achieve well-being.

Once health had been defined, the multi-faceted nature of the strategies that would be required to improve health became apparent to the Council. A wealth of documentation was reviewed and a wide variety of agencies and organisations were met to ensure that Council members were up to date with the views and perspectives on health and health care in the province. In addition the health goals committee met with the Deputy Ministers of those departments which would be involved in a comprehensive health plan. As a result of these activities the Council adopted a draft 'Comprehensive Health Strategy' which set out the complexity of reviewing planning and delivering health services and which was widely distributed for public review and consultation.

The strategy suggested nine essential policy considerations: health status enhancement; the health care system; social policy; physical environment issues; collaboration and participation; technology assessment; innovation and evaluation; intergovernmental programmes and resource allocation and acquisition policy. Against this background, the Council released a discussion paper in April 1992 entitled *Developing Health Goals and a Comprehensive Health Strategy for Nova Scotia*, as well as a draft summary version of the paper. This was distributed throughout the province to community organisations, providers, the general public, government departments, agencies, advocacy groups, elected representatives and public libraries. Public meetings, advertised in newspapers, posters and household flyers, were held and at each meeting the chairperson of the Council, the executive director and one or more members were present. A questionnaire was also provided with the discussion paper for written submissions and a toll free telephone line was also set up.

The draft health goals were revised according to the advice received from the public and formal organisations and were approved by the government in August 1992. The process of how the goals were changed from the initial draft as a result of consultative processes and the main themes and issues of each goal were then published in a report at the end of 1992.[25] Health goals are broad statements concerning what Nova Scotians want health, and the health care system to be like in the future. They are an overall set of directions, not a list of specific targets, that will serve as guideposts for better planning decisions at all levels, including the Regional Health Agencies and government departments. Health goals are also intended to make it easier to evaluate planning decisions and assess the progress made. The goals encompass health promotion, a healthy environment, support for healthy living, wise and equitable management of resources, participation in decisions affecting health and the proper consideration of social factors which affect physical and mental welfare. Significantly, as the health care system is regarded as only a part of the larger health picture, Nova Scotia's health goals are not based solely on a medical model of health and have a much wider ambit than health *care*.

The next step for the Council was to make recommendations for beginning the process of moving towards the attainment of the province's health goals by initiating reform. In addition to the advice received in the health goal round of consultations, the Council's recommendations were based on recent studies and initiatives at national level and in other provinces. This initial action plan consisted of 51 recommendations organised according to the six Health Goals but concentrating for the most part on the management and participation goals. The recommendations were organised under the three main headings: immediate action points; areas requiring greater

---

25 Nova Scotias Health Goals: how they were developed and what they mean (Provincial Health Council, December 1992).

accountability to the public and areas requiring further public input. The Department of Health was asked to respond and to indicate how and when it would address each recommendation.

The Provincial Health Council had worked tirelessly and really taken to heart the role set it by government. Besides health reform there were also a number of other issues with which the Council was involved in its early days, including the lack of information and consultation on the feasibility of capital expenditure on the hospital rebuilding programme and access to tobacco products by children.[26]

In its publication on community participation the Strengthening Community Health Partnership found that the Provincial Health Council had developed credibility by involving Nova Scotians in health planning and by providing reliable information about the health system. It was agreed that achievement of the health goals depended on stronger links between health planning bodies. Because health cut across traditional departmental boundaries, to facilitate collaboration it was felt that the Council should report directly to the provincial Cabinet rather than the Minister of Health, and there should be the same geographical service boundaries for all government departments. There was also a need to expand and legitimise the role of the Council. To carry out its function effectively the Council must be assured of adequate funding for communication, staff and research as well as reliable and full access to information.

Regional Health Agencies

Both the Royal Commission and the Department of Health's *Health Strategy for the Nineties* had recommended the adoption of a regional planning system as one of the fundamental administrative changes necessary to improve the efficiency and effectiveness of health services in Nova Scotia. The phased introduction of Regional Health Agencies was announced in May 1992.[27]

The main purpose of Regional Health Agencies was stated to be to advise the Minister of Health on health and health care issues for their respective regions and to recommend positive changes in the health care system. They were to provide community based input on ways to improve the health of the population. They would also review health issues referred to them by the Minister for discussion and advice.

---

26 'As a result of the Council's recommendations the legal age for purchase of tobacco products was raised to 19 years amongst other measures.

27 *An Introduction to Regional Health Agencies; public participation in health care planning* (Nova Scotia Department of Health, 1992).

Regional Health Agencies (RHA) would comprise a group of people appointed by the Minister of Health. Members would volunteer their time and expertise to work with health organisations and the public and must be widely representative. There were to be 12-18 members on each RHA which would report directly to the Minister of Health. The Board must have an equitable balance of health care users (including community group volunteers), providers (including health professionals), and health advocates. Whilst each member was to be valued for his or her knowledge and experience, each was to function as *a representative of the public*. The chairperson was to be appointed for a three year term and initially the length of service of other members was to be staggered to ensure continuity of Agency membership. Once out of this initial stage, one third of membership will be reappointed each year. Each member may only serve a maximum of two terms. Each was to have a staff of two or three persons: a Regional Co-ordinator plus one or two support staff.

In accordance with health goals approved by government and consistent with policies, guidelines and standards set by the Department of Health, the overall mandate of RHAs was to:

- develop an ongoing regional health plan in consultation with the public and health service providers which encompasses all health care programmes. It was anticipated that the plan would identify and address local community health needs and priorities; recommend ways of increasing the effectiveness and efficiency of the health care system in the region; recommend ways to foster greater co-ordination and integration of health services; and promote co-operation among service providers and consumers;

- consult with the Provincial Health Council regarding health goals and how to achieve them, to assist in enhancing public awareness and encouraging public input regarding the same;

- enhance public awareness of health issues, the challenges facing the health care system and the need for change;

- recommend ways of improving population health in their region within available resource;

- provide advice on matters referred by the Minister of Health.

In view of the complexity of the implementation process, it was expected that RHAs would not be able immediately to fulfil all aspects of their mandate, but it was anticipated that each Agency should develop its health plan within three years of being established. Each Agency would be required to provide an annual report to the Minister outlining its activities and progress towards completion of their plan. Subsequent to the initial plan being completed for each region, all proposed major adjustments in health care service infrastructure and funding would be reviewed by the Department and then commented on by the relevant Agency. It was anticipated that once initial regional plans were finalised they would become the primary focal point for the Minister of Health in reviewing and monitoring regional health systems. The Minister of Health stated it was expected that RHA recommendations would be based on a prudent look at needs, health care resources and available financial resources. It was also expected that advice to the Minister would take account of the current and future fiscal situation of the province and would consider means of reorganisation of resources rather than requests for new services. In other words RHAs would be responsible for containing costs.

Consequent on the complexity of the task set for RHAs (the Department of Health acknowledged that its scope appeared intimidating) it was important for them to develop both formal and informal channels of communication with providers, health care agencies and consumers within the region. A number of regional health planning and delivery agencies existed prior to the introduction of RHAs, in service areas such as Mental Health, Drug Dependency and Community Health which RHAs would have to harness.

It was also important that RHAs would benefit from communication amongst themselves to avoid duplication of effort in information gathering and other initiatives and gain from one anothers experience. RHAs would be able to tap into Department of Health information and resources on a regular basis, particularly that within the Policy, Planning and Research Division.

However, the Provincial Health Council indicated concern about the growing number of regional and local health related planning bodies which could make it impossible for any one group, particularly the RHAs, to function effectively.[28] The Council identified a whole range of groups including the regional hospital planning committees, local drug dependency committees, inter-agency councils, multi-service centres, and the proposed regional mental health planning boards. The Council believed that for effective planning to occur there had to be formal relationships and co-ordination between RHAs and other groups. This was not possible with such multiplicity and consequently there was recommended amalgamation of all regional planning activities and resources under the Regional Health Agencies.

Whilst recognising the significance of Regional Health Agencies as an important step towards decentralisation and collaborative health

---

28 *Towards Achieving Nova Scotia's Health Goals: An Initial Plan for Action for Health Care Reform* (Provincial Health Council, December 1992).

planning, there were persistent calls for RHAs to be more representative of the communities they served and for the people of those communities to be involved in developing criteria for selecting members and in the selection process itself. Concern was also expressed about the degree to which RHAs could actually make and implement decisions about spending in their region.[29] Further, members of the three RHAs which were actually established expressed frustration at the lack of support they received in taking on the responsibility. Members felt that they needed guidance on the development of common definitions, knowledge, visions and language and in the skills required for community participation. It was strongly suggested that RHAs would be more effective if formally linked to one another and the Provincial Health Council, rather than functioning in isolation. These contentions were also reiterated by the Provincial Health Council who pointed out that there needed to be a clear statement of what was expected of those appointed to RHAs. It was also stated that it was unreasonable to expect that one professional staff person assisted by one or two support staff could be expected to sustain the expected activities of a RHA.

Subsequently, at the request of the Minister of Health the Provincial Health Council met with representatives from the existing RHAs to discuss how the agencies might evolve into operational authorities. A resultant discussion paper on Regional Health Authorities and community health, describing the processes needed to decentralise the health system, was circulated to the Department of Health and the RHAs for comments.

Hospital organisation

As yet in this chapter little has been said about the position of hospitals. Hospitals in Canada are for the most part owned by charities and municipalities. In Nova Scotia, which is typical of the rest of Canada, there are around 52 hospitals and other health facilities owned by the municipalities, religious orders, private not-for-profit and for-profit organisations.

The Hospitals Act and the Health Services and Insurance Act govern the operation of these hospitals and the Department of Health has responsibility for funding transfer payments to them. For the purposes of planning and reviewing hospital services the province is

---

29 *A Framework for Action, Community Participation in Health Planning in Nova Scotia* (The Strengthening Community Health Partnership, 1993). The Partnership is a national programme supported by the federal Department of Health and Welfare.

divided into six regions and there are also internal Department of Health consultants for each major functional area such as nursing, diagnostic services, support services and so on. Of the 44 facilities that could be eligible, 36 have participated in the Canadian Council on Health Facilities and the other eight have received or will receive service reviews by the Department of Health to help them achieve accreditation status.

The Hospitals Act vests responsibility for the actual governance of health care facilities in a board of trustees. The board is legally and morally responsible for the institution and the service it provides. The board's major role is to ensure that adequate and proper health care services are delivered in a quality manner consistent with community needs. The role of trustees is based on a firm belief that policy decisions are best made by local citizens who have no vested interest in the affairs of the facility. Consequently it is fundamental that the system is maintained and only 'interested, dedicated and motivated people are considered for recruitment onto boards'.[30]

The trustee board system which is common throughout Canada provides an opportunity for the devolution of decision-making about hospital services to the local level. There is a clear separation between trustees and chief executive and other managers who see themselves as agents of the board. Although trustees are not generally directly elected their appointment is more open and taken from a wider public than has been the case with the appointment of non-executive members of National Health Service (NHS) trusts in the UK. Only trustees have a right to vote on policy which may be introduced by trustees or by the chief executive for consideration. To supplement information for trustees, workshops and conferences which address specific issues are held regularly to take account of public perceptions.

Recent developments are of course causing changes to the role and powers of hospital trustees which are currently being negotiated and in some instances jealously guarded. Some of the wider powers relating to the development and introduction of services that hospital trustees have enjoyed are being transferred to regional and community health bodies to deter duplication, ineffective health care interventions and assist planning. Although in many cases across Canada informal forums have sought this objective, they have not always been particularly successful. However the model of the trustee board is for the most part being preserved at regional and community level.

The fundamental difference between the NHS Trust and the Canadian boards is hard to define, but is perhaps best articulated in

---

30   Association of Health Organisations, *Me! ... a Trustee?*

terms of approach or ethos and is very much related to constitutional underpinnings and expectations of openness and participation in government. This difference is reflected in the nomenclature, role emphasis, appointment, training and support and the provision of information to boards. In Canada there has been a recognition that the financial and quality care issues of the future are likely to place stress on the voluntary governance system. In consequence, consideration has been given by most provinces to the need to develop, promote and implement a process and structure which enhances the effectiveness of trustees. A review of trusteeship undertaken in Nova Scotia has been accepted in other provinces and guidelines have been issued or are in the process of being taken into account in relation to the concerns mentioned. One of the most challenging aspects of trusteeship, to understand and negotiate the *interaction* between governance and management, has been carefully addressed. the two roles are seen as complementary but different to each other, to the health organisation and the community. A code of guidance has been established which sets out the two roles in terms of planning, finance, quality of care and organisation. There is also provision for the review of the effectiveness of trustee boards in the national accreditation scheme for health care facilities.

Canadian boards thus have a very different focus to their NHS counterparts. Canadian trustees see their role as very much a part of local democracy, accountable to the local community for the strategy and delivery of effective health care. The role of management in hospitals is to put that strategy into practice in an efficient and economically viable manner. Trustees are for the most part appointed after an open and well publicised campaign as it is regarded as desirable to avoid elections to keep hospital governance out of the political arena. Current trustees and the chair ensure that the various factions of the community are properly represented and reflect the demographic contour of the area in respect of race, age, gender.

In the UK there has been more of an overall emphasis on financial concerns and less consideration of representation of the community.[31] In the UK the role of board meetings tends to be seen more as a means of keeping non-executive directors informed of decisions taken elsewhere, rather than for extensive formulation and discussion of policy. The unitary boards seem to offer little opportunity for non-executive directors to hold management to account as the former are often at a disadvantage in terms of knowledge and information and are

---

31 This focus is reflected in the report *Public Enterprise Governance in the NHS and the Codes on Conduct and Accountability for NHS boards.* See Chapter 4 pp 120–122.

seen as interfering with management. Their role was not as clearly defined as in Canada and did not allow the kind of independent evaluation that has been institutionalised in the Canadian system.

The codes of conduct and accountability set out by the UK Department of Health are designed for the most part to strengthen probity and financial control; to promote the stewardship of public funds. There has been little attempt to insert any of the enhanced requirements for appointment, training and support that are evident in the Canadian codes which render their boards generally more responsive to the community than their UK counterparts. Canadian provincial governments are also far more ready to acknowledge shortfalls and change legislation to counteract criticism and maintain the constitutional balance.

In late 1992 the Auditor General of Nova Scotia conducted a review of accountability for hospitals at the Department of Health.[32] It was concluded in that report that there were deficiencies in the accountability framework for hospitals relating to the setting of objectives and reporting performance in attaining objectives. These deficiencies pertained to both the relationship between hospitals and the Department of Health, and between the Department, the Executive Council and the Legislature. In addition, although the Department of Health's annual report complied with the current government Management Manual, the Auditor General regarded it as inadequate as an accountability document. However, the Department's systems for monitoring, controlling and reporting of hospital activities was regarded as very good.

The report considered that there should be an accountability framework which encompassed all bodies responsible for different aspects of the provision of hospital services in the province and which clearly defined their roles, authority and responsibility. This framework would involve mechanisms for setting objectives, contracting, reporting and taking corrective action. It was suggested that the Department of Health should address the Royal Commission's recommendations and report its progress to the legislature at appropriate intervals, a key issue was that insufficient information flowed to the legislature to enable it to determine whether its objectives had been met. The report recognised that some progress had in fact been made, but despite this one of the main accountability recommendations of the Royal Commission had not been addressed:

> That effective planning, financial management, and accountability be
> strengthened in view of projected demands on the health care system

---

32   *Health – Accountability and Hospitals* (Report of the Auditor General, 1992).

and of the provincial economic climate. That targeted levels of health spending be established globally and for individual programmes within the health budget.[33]

The specific responsibility of hospitals is defined mainly through the hospital Reference Manual and more informally through contact with Department regional officers. The responsibilities defined dealt primarily with financial and statistical requirements. The Auditor General stated that he would like to see better provisions relating to objectives and performance expectations set out in legislation to try to ensure consistency amongst hospitals. In effect the Auditor General was recommending something akin to the social contract suggested by the Steering Committee for Review of the Ontario Public Hospitals Act.[34]

The Auditor also pointed out that s 19 of the Hospitals Act permitted the government to appoint one member to each hospital board, but there were no terms of reference for members appointed in such a way. It appeared that the government had not considered this opportunity of influencing hospital administration and operation.

The Auditor also recommended that hospitals should develop mission statements and strategic plans in conjunction with the Department of Health. The report concluded that although the Provincial Health Council had indicated that its reporting relationship with the Minister of Health had not presented any difficulties, it felt that it should have its accountability set out formally so as to avoid potential problems. Clarification of the Council's mandate and degree of priority assigned to its various functions was also needed.

The Auditor was also critical of the lack of any long-term strategic plan within the Department and the lack of an accountability framework for the Provincial Health Council and the Regional Health Agencies. Although the Department of Health had made progress in implementing the Royal Commission on Health Care's recommendations, further strengthening of accountability was required through preparation of a detailed blue print for health reform as advocated by the Commission and the Provincial Health Council.

The report was also critical of the Department of Health's decision that RHAs should be advisory bodies only and the potential overlap of the respective roles and responsibilities of RHAs and Regional Hospital Planning Committees needed to be clarified.

Management of the Department of Health however, informed the Auditor General that there was work in progress on a strategic plan

---

33 Royal Commission Report, recommendation 6.03 quoted *ibid* at 15.32.

34 *Into the 21st Century, Ontario Public Hospitals* (February 1992).

but that the Department had decided to await the tabling of the objectives of the Provincial Health Council before completion of its own document.

The Nova Scotia Association of Health Organisations

As the Auditor General criticised the lack of progress towards the reforms and the short-comings of those already in place, perhaps surprisingly, the Nova Scotia Association of Health Organisations (AHO) threw its weight behind increased public participation and greater emphasis on primary care.

The AHO was incorporated in 1960 and is a not-for-profit independent organisation representing and serving the interests of member hospitals, homes for special care, community health clinics, rehabilitation centres, and other health care organisations and agencies. The AHO function is to promote an effective, efficient, and integrated quality health system throughout the province through:

- leadership in influencing the development of public policy;
- representing and advocating members interests;
- providing services to assist members to meet the health care needs of their communities.[35]

As part of its role the AHO liaises with organisations at provincial and national level and participates in the activities and decision-making processes of the Canadian Hospital Association, the Canadian Council on Health Facilities Accreditation and federal and provincial government bodies. Its Education, Research and Communication Division designs and conducts research activities to formulate AHO positions and monitors the political, social and health care environments to identify issues, changes and trends in support of the Association's objectives.

The AHO Statement of Values is interesting because it is quite removed from what might be expected of an organisation of health care providers, particularly in the current commercial orientation of the UK and New Zealand. The AHO believe in the joint responsibility of the public, health providers and government for the prudent use of resources and a common integrated set of goals and objectives to drive the health system. They believe that members of the Association have an obligation to subscribe to *responsible* corporate values and that

---

35   Nova Scotia Association of Health Organisations, *Mission Statement* (1993).

public participation through the voluntary governance of health care programmes is an essential component of public accountability.[36]

To this latter end the AHO resolved in 1990 to develop, promote and implement a process and structure to enhance hospital trustee effectiveness. It commissioned a study of the reality of trustee contributions in order to recommend ways of improving individual and collective input.[37] The report identified a number of areas in which the AHO could lend its support and the AHO established a task force to report on the study and develop an action plan for implementation.[38] This established a statement on the function of trustees and documented the relationship between the trustee role of governance and the different role of management, the vital point being that the two were complementary to each other, the organisation and to the community.

This position on trusteeship, set out for the AHO the generic principles to be applied to all health boards and formed one of the cornerstones of their recommendations for the future structure of the health system in Nova Scotia.[39]

In their report the AHO called for a new way of thinking about the health system, the role of providers within the system and the way providers interrelated with others in the region and communities. The 'New Paradigm' followed quite closely the principles of the Royal Commission, the four main tenets were: enhancing public participation; integration of health care through the establishment of community health boards; decentralisation of planning and delivery and reinforcement of the strategic role of the Department of Health in health policy development.

The AHO noted that the level of participation in health care decision making is the extent to which individuals have control over the decision-making process. Informing was insufficient if no channels for feedback were supplied or there was no possibility for negotiation or sharing of planning and responsibility. The AHO advocated community development as a strategy to enhance participation by developing partnerships to allow communities to organise themselves to solve problems. This highlighted issues such as the appointment or election of boards, how representative boards were of their communities, the influence health professionals exert on the decision-

---

36 NSAHO *Statement of Values* (1993).

37 *Enhancing Hospital Governance* (Thomas Regan Acadia University, 1991).

38 *Position on Trusteeship* (NSAHO, November 1992).

39 *The New Paradigm: A new system structure and organisation for health services delivery in Nova Scotia* (NSAHO, June 1993).

making process, the preparedness of board members and the communication channels between a board and its community, all of which have a greater impact on participation than the actual number of boards. The AHO stated that providers and government needed to move out of the paternalistic mode and build new skills and seek out new mechanisms.

The AHO also believed that all health care organisations should have an extended role in primary care as they consider an appropriate balance of treatment, prevention promotion, rehabilitation and support activities are the key to effective health care. In particular they saw a potential for small community hospitals to become a nucleus for primary health care in their communities. These organisations have the infrastructure and identity to evolve, from the hospital acute care model, to community health centres or multi-service centres. They also have a potential to become facilitators of the community development process central to primary health. The community health board would replace existing independent board structures.[40] The creation of a single board to deliver a mix of health services is a significant new concept in Nova Scotia and is seen as having the potential to become the foundation of the whole health system. Within this system trustees would find the focus changed from health care to health and from individual organisations to the health status of their community. The AHO believe that this presents the opportunity to bring the voluntary trusteeship system of governance to its full potential.

The third tenet of the new paradigm, that of decentralisation, had initially been unacceptable to the AHO. But it was now regarded by the Association as an essential component of public accountability. The Association subscribes to decentralisation of planning, programme delivery and funding authority from government to regional bodies that would be responsible for the provision of an integrated continuum of care to a regional population. Due to the wide distribution of the provinces relatively small population base, most communities are unable to efficiently and effectively provide a full range of health services and rely on other communities within or outwith their respective region to provide services. A regional authority could match needs to resources. The Regional Authority according to the AHO would be a composite of the community boards of the region so that all communities would have the opportunities to act as advocates of their respective needs. Additional members could be elected by the regional community. The regional authority would have the difficult task of balancing primary, secondary and tertiary care. These authorities

---

40 The AHO recognised that in the larger urban areas the size and complexity of organisations might require a specific study and step by step approach.

would be considerably different from the Regional Health Agencies currently being set up and would require strong administrative support to fulfil their role. The AHO believe that the region should also take responsibility for the other regional co-ordinated programmes for mental health, drug dependency and community health.

The Department of Health would be responsible for ensuring the province develops a system that operates within the context of national goals and ensures the maintenance of the Canada Health Act. It would also develop overall strategy and public policy, establish the core programmes for health and provide the tools and process to support effective management of the system and set provincial standards and guidelines.

The AHO believes that this structure will eliminate unnecessary duplication, provide a seamless, integrated health system that allows individuals to enter at a point appropriate to their needs and provide co-ordinated management structures. They have acknowledged that such restructuring would not be easy, but are convinced that the governance and management structures of Nova Scotia must evolve in relation to the changing need of the provinces communities and in partnership with other health providers.

The blueprint for the way forward

The government of Nova Scotia finally began to respond to the mounting criticism and urging of the Provincial Health Council in November 1993 when the Minister of Health appointed an Action Committee on Health System Reform which brought together a cross section of citizens with a rich diversity of skills and perspectives that included health care consumers, providers, administrators, researchers, educators, advocates and trustees. The task of this 'Blueprint Committee' as it became known, was to develop a framework to guide the overall restructuring of the province's health system. The Provincial Health Council, after extensive discussions with the Minister of Health, agreed to play a lead role in the development of the Blueprint as long as it was developed in consultation with the public and the Council was able to retain its independence and later comment on the Blueprint and its implementation.

The Blueprint Committee addressed every major aspect of the health care system and consulted widely before publishing a framework for its renovation. The Committee's Report was published in April 1994[41] and was well received. The Committee supported collective and individual choice and recommended that the reformed

---

41   *Nova Scotia's Blueprint for Health System Reform.*

health care system should be built from the community up, through a network of community health boards (CHB), four Regional Health Boards (RHB) and a Provincial Programs Advisory Committee (PPAC) The purpose of RHBs was to plan, fund, co-ordinate and evaluate programs for their region. Four interim boards made up of no less than two thirds consumers should be established to facilitate the setting up of community boards. Once community health boards CHBs were in place permanent regional health boards RHBs could follow. Two thirds of the representatives of each of these should be nominated by the CHBs, the remaining third to be appointed by the Minister of Health.

The purpose of CHBs would be to plan, fund, co-ordinate and evaluate all primary care and to be the driving force behind community development. The Committee recognised that there were strong arguments supporting both election and appointment to these boards and recommended that this should be resolved by public discussion. In any event, consumers should make up at least half the membership.

The PPAC, with representatives of each of the four regions, the Department of Health and other, non governmental organisations would plan, co-ordinate and evaluate provincial programmes. The Committee also recommended an expanded 'watchdog' role for the Provincial Health Council with greater capacity to consult and inform the public on matters relating to health. It was also to assist in developing objectives and targets for health goals and design a health impact assessment tool so that all public policy could be analysed to determine health implications. This would hold government, departments and agencies publicly accountable for the extent to which health public policy was supported in decision-making.

This would be underlined by a new Council reporting relationship to the legislature, through the Premier, as opposed to the Minister of Health as presently the case. This was seen as consistent with the multi-departmental nature of public health policy and would give the Council a more comprehensive insight into government activities.

The Department of Health took another twelve months to produce a plan in reply to the Blueprint Committee's proposals. At one time the Provincial Health Council feared that the entire process was in danger of being derailed. Although changes were under way in a number of key areas the Regional and Community Health Boards Act which had been going through the Nova Scotia legislature at the time the Blueprint Committee were deliberating needed revision if it was to create more than two new levels of bureaucracy. In addition information on health system reform was not being communicated to the public on a regular basis.

From Blueprint to Building[42] is the most comprehensive report to date on the Nova Scotian Department of Health efforts to reform the health system. On the positive side, as well as making several references to the Blueprint it reaffirms that the Department is committed to communicating the renewal of the provinces health system to the public.[43] However the report fails to adequately address some of the serious issues and concerns about the government's approach to health system reform raised by the Provincial Health Council and others and it is frequently inconsistent with the *Blueprint*.

The Council listed nearly 40 factors in the Department of Health's proposals which were at variance with the *Blueprint* Report. Essentially it was unclear as to what aspects of the *Blueprint* were endorsed by the Department and what were not. The report was vague about its processes of communication and consultation. There was no mention of the potential impact of recently announced changes to federal funding arrangements nor the funding 'envelopes' which were recommended in the earlier document to allow communities and regions to finance their own initiatives. The proposed reforms were not set in the context of Nova Scotia's health goals or *Blueprint* principles. Community development which was the essence of the *Blueprint* reforms was totally neglected. There was little to foster the role of volunteers or support informal care givers and minimal reference was made to the input of non-governmental organisation, all of which was regarded as paramount by the *Blueprint* Committee. The scope of primary health care was narrow and health promotion was inadequately addressed given the inherent changing philosophy in health reform.

As regards the organisational structure, the Department proposals conveyed a top-down approach to community involvement which was not in keeping with the spirit of the *Blueprint*. It placed emphasis on service delivery and developing regional plans rather than the establishment of CHBs. *Blueprint* had clearly articulated the conflict that would arise if both RHBs and CHBs were allowed to deliver services. But the Department's report stated that this would indeed be the case. Nor was there any reference to the deficiencies of the Regional Health Boards Act or the process underway to review it.

Lastly it was suggested that the role of the suggested Provincial Programs and Services Board should be narrowed and that the Provincial Health Council be subsumed by a Health Research

---

42 *Renovating Nova Scotia's Health System* (Department of Health, April 1995).
43 Provincial Health Council letter to the Minister of Health (31 July 1995).

Foundation which would consider public health policy and the Council's current mandate.

The Department of Health's proposals were stated to be developed to preserve those parts of the system that were working well, while changing the components which needed to be improved. It was also developed in full recognition and support of the government's plan for fiscal recovery. Under the Financial Measures Act (1994) responsibility is placed on the government of Nova Scotia to present a balanced budget by 1998. It is arguable that this is currently the paramount matter where health sector reform is concerned.

The transfer of jurisdictional responsibility from the provinces hospital boards to the Regional Health Boards was to have begun early in 1995, but was postponed until later in the year. Indications are that there may be a further postponement. Responsibility for home care and public health is to be phased into the regional structure over the next two years and long term care to come under the Regional Health Boards in 1998. The latter is already under-resourced to meet the needs of residents and has experienced additional stresses due to the reduction of the hospital sector and the reductions that the provincial government has made to the health budget.[44]

The AHO and several other organisations are now actively involved in an organised review of the Health Boards Act 1994 which is seeking to clarify the relationship between Regional and Community Health Boards and public accountability of health care organisations.

BRITISH COLUMBIA

In March 1990 the Royal Commission on Health Care and Costs began an extensive 20 month examination of health services in British Columbia which employs more than 60,000 people and costs well over three quarters of a million dollars an hour. Its goal was to determine how the current system worked in the climate of minimal or even no scope for overall expansion of government expenditure, and what could be done to improve it. In November 1991 the Commission released a three volume report *Closer to Home*.

The Commission was unanimous in their opinion that the British Columbian health system was 'one of the best, and quite possibly the best, in the world'. But there was room for improvement and this would mean resetting priorities, reallocating funds and removing barriers to effective health care.

---

44   *Community Continuing Care, A New Horizon* (1994) and the Response of NSAHO (1994).

... too often needs go unmet. Too often creative and cost-effective solutions to health care problems – particularly problems in the delivery of services – are opposed by a fortress mentality that equates change with threat, shifts in priorities or reallocation of funds with cutbacks and integration and accountability with loss of control.[45]

Although the Commission recognised the WHO definition of health and that the social and economic environment is a critical determinant of human health they concentrated on the fields set out in their terms of reference and consequent reform of the structure of the health care system. The Commission believed that their recommendations were both pragmatic in nature and achievable in scope.

The Commission reaffirmed their commitment to the principles of the Canada Health Act and pointed out that although every province had taken steps to discourage or prevent extra-billing and has removed hospital user fees, no province had gone further. Thus it was important that the government of British Columbia take the first step to make these principles an integral part of British Columbia law.

Through consultation the Commission arrived at a set of guidelines which along with the national Medicare principles were regarded as necessary components to a health care system.

- *Closer to Home*. Medically necessary services must be provided in, or as near to, the patients place of residence as is consistent with quality and cost-effective health care.

- *The Public First*. Public servants and professionals must always put the public interest ahead of their own or their members interests.

- *Outcomes*. The focus of the health care system must be on providing those services which improve health outcomes. These outcomes must be defined, measurable, subject to analysis and be able to be independently evaluated. Services which cannot be shown to improve health should not be funded by the health care system.

- *Community Involvement*. Decisions should be made as close to the community level as possible; local people must be allowed to shape the local system of health delivery services. Government should be prepared to fund co-ordination and to encourage the creation of advisory boards. But if government attempts to force citizens to participate in schemes designed by the Ministry of Health the boards will be failures.

- *Funding*. The health system must be reformed within the current levels of spending. At the same time, government must recognise

---

45   *Closer to Home* (Province of British Columbia, Vol 1) p 5.

that although provincial revenues may vary, sickness does not. There must be less variability in the funding of health care than there is in other areas.

- *The Jericho Process.* Administrative walls within the Ministry of Health, among all ministries, health care institutions and organisations and between all of these groups and educational institutions, must be broken down in favour of an integrated health system.

- *Necessary Education.* All tasks within the health system should be open to people with the education necessary to provide high quality care. People should not be barred from performing a task because they lack education which is necessary to performing that task and does not demonstrably improve health outcomes. The 'credentialisation' of positions within the health care system must be stopped.

- *Volunteers.* Citizens who volunteer help are a significant part of the health care system and are vital to developing new programmes. People have the right to participate directly by volunteering their time in appropriate roles that include governance, patient service and advocacy, but not by replacing paid staff. Neither should paid staff or their representatives seek to replace volunteers. Volunteers should have some control over the jobs that they do. During labour disputes, essential service agreements should identify appropriate volunteer roles.

- *Openness.* Except where privacy and confidentiality demand otherwise, all information on health and health care gathered by public servants in ministries and publicly funded institutions should be available to the public and to researchers. Secrecy breeds suspicion and shows a lack of respect for the public. Openness can foster credibility, understanding and acceptance.

The Commission commented that in the present economic climate and the decline or possible disappearance of federal support any expansion of programmes in health care would necessitate shifting resources from other areas. The record suggested however that transferring resources is difficult. Even pronounced changes within the health care sector tended to be cancelled out over time.[46] Rigid patterns could not be allowed to continue if new priorities of need were to be met. This entailed transferring funds over time from the acute sector to

---

46 The Commission referred amongst other things to past attempts to reallocate a percentage of the provincial health budget from hospitals to physicians. This had been reversed slowly over less than 10 years.

continuing care, home care and other less intensive institutional and residential provision.[47] The Commission were critical that there had never been any overall plan for health services; the structure that had evolved lacked coherence and sometimes logic. They consequently recommended the setting up of a permanent independent Provincial Health Council to oversee the total health care system and be able to review policies, plans and programmes of the Ministry of Health and any other public or private body whose action affected the health of the province. The Council should be able to inform the public of how well the government is meeting health care needs and bring its influence to bear on difficult high profile issues. The role of the Council would be to:

- enunciate specific goals for the health care system;
- evaluate information to determine the degree of progress in reaching these goals;
- advise the government, when requested or on its own initiative, on contentious issues;
- review and comment on the health policies and plans of the Ministry of Health;
- assess the effectiveness of all parts of the health care system, including the evaluation component;
- ensure that authoritative health information is easily available to the public;
- direct the provincial health officer to investigate or research public health concerns.

If the Council was to have authority and credibility, its members must be independent, objective and influential, have security of tenure, a small staff and the power to contract for services and the responsibility to make an annual report. They would also need access to all the information available to the Ministry of Health and other ministries, institutions and organisations. However the Commission affirmed the ultimate power of the legislature to make decisions about the health system and recommended that the Council be accountable to the legislature, not the Ministry of Health.

The Commission was critical of the lack of information on which to assess whether a particular health intervention was of value or not and there were no standard grounds on which to base professional reviews or compare the performance of different institutions. In fact there was

47 Hospitals consume almost half the Province's budget.

also little evaluation of the information that was collected, whether it was accurate, useful and in a form to enable solutions to be found to problems. All too often:

> Collecting information becomes an end in itself and pertinent facts are ignored in favour of inaction or political expediency.[48]

There needed to be established common accounting guidelines for comparing costs and a public mandate for each hospital and clinic for the services they would provide and population they would serve. The Ministry of Health should be enabled to reduce funding to those institutions which did not fulfil their mandate. Mandates however would not be subject to change without public consultation.

The Commission found that the present system of centralised management had failed the public in that it was insensitive to local and regional questions, inflexible in its programmes and policies and unfair in its distribution of resources. It did not encourage those it funded or served to participate in the control of the system. Whilst proposals for operating budgets came from hospitals and local communities, all of the monetary decisions were taken in the Ministry of Health. They recommended that the province be divided into several health regions and each be assigned a funding envelope containing all of the health care dollars for that region with the exception of funding for programmes administered province-wide.

They also supported the creation of local and community boards to advise regional general managers on the allocation of resources in their area. It was also considered that regional budgets should be published to encourage and allow time for consumer and provider groups to advocate changes.

It was also noted that alternative health service delivery means such as community health organisations had had little success in establishing themselves in British Columbia. In the light of evidence that physician opposition to alternative methods of delivery was fading and hospitalisation might be reduced there should be active support for alternatives through co-ordination of policies, procedures and possibly legislation.

There was immediate criticism of the Royal Commissions recommendations for regionalisation from the British Columbia Hospital Association (BCHA).[49] The aim of their report was to identify the factors that had affected the success or failure of regionalisation and determine how those factors might apply to regional governance in

---

48 *ibid.*

49 *Regionalisation in the Delivery of Health Care: an Analysis of Implementation Strategies* (BCHA, July 1992).

British Columbia. The BCHA found that there was little consensus on what regionalisation meant, although there were three common characteristics, decentralisation, geographic organisation and rationalisation. The impetus for regionalisation could be social and political reasons, scientific and technological reasons or managerial and economic reasons. They argued that regionalisation was often seen as a panacea for all that ails a health care system and they reported on the attempts to regionalise in other jurisdictions, including the UK and New Zealand. The BCHA identified a number of criteria which most affected success; clarity of vision, political will, legislation, resistance by stakeholders and the implementation process. They also identified a lack of available information about whether regionalisation had achieved its intended goals and lack of data by which to measure this. Based on the experience of other governments, a number of issues needed to be dealt with if regionalisation was to be achieved. There needed to be a clear plan, and a mutually adaptive approach needed to be adopted so that regions could emerge through a process of self determination. The Minister would have to ensure that resistance from those implementing the strategy was overcome and the changes needed to be enshrined in legislation.

The working group that the Minister had set up to address the concept of regionalisation was seen as a positive step towards mutual adaptation, but discussions had involved too small a group of stakeholders.

The government of British Columbia responded to the Royal Commission by setting up a 25 member advisory committee which consulted with key professional and voluntary participants in the health sector over a period of ten months. In creating their plan for a renewed health system the Ministry of Health established a foundation from which changes and priorities flowed.[50] The foundation established a definition of health which crafted a vision of what a revitalised health system should look like on which all common decisions would be based.

The government endorsed the WHO definition of health as a resource for everyday life, emphasising personal and social resources. Accordingly the shared vision of health in British Columbia was one of healthy citizens – taking personal responsibility and able financially and socially to make informed and effective decisions and choices regarding their health and wise use of the health system and health

---

50 *New Directions for a Healthy British Columbia: meeting the challenge* (Ministry of Health and Ministry Responsible for Seniors, British Columbia, February 1993).

communities – characterised by local government, business, labour and other citizens working together to identify and resolve social, ecological and economic realities affecting health.

The government then set out five new directions supported by priority actions which paid particular regard to equity, partnership, financial responsibility and sensitive implementation. These directions were:

- *Better health.* More attention would be paid to factors that affected the state of health, income, housing, environment. Health promotion and disease prevention programmes would be fostered and community action strengthened by harnessing not only federal and local governments and health care providers, but business, schools, labour and communities as well as families and individuals.

  To ensure a focus on better health a provincial health council would be set up to promote public awareness about health issues and review and report publicly on matters affecting health. A clear set of health goals would be established and a new provincial health officer would be appointed to monitor emerging health issues and carry out specific health promotion and prevention activities.

  To deal with obstacles to equitable service and status specific health policy frameworks would be developed for particular disadvantaged groups and health impact assessments would be made part of the approval process for any new government policy or legislation.

- *Greater public participation and accountability.* Public representation would be increased on professional regulatory boards and there would be greater opportunity for local decision-making by citizens.

  The public would be provided with more information and opportunity to use it. A Freedom of Information Act and Protection of Privacy Act would be implemented. The Ombudsman Act (1992) would be extended to cover hospitals, hospital boards and government of professional bodies. Legislation would be amended to ensure that lay representatives would constitute at least one third of all professional governance bodies. Patients would have access to their own medical records and a health information network would be established to provide information to the public, physicians and pharmacists on specific concerns and information would be distributed about health care costs and the appropriate use of health services.

- *Bringing health closer to home.* In order to endorse the main criticism made by the Royal Commission of over centralisation, three major reforms were required which would take a consultative, developmental approach.

  Community Health Councils and Regional Health Boards would be developed and the necessary enabling legislation prepared. 'Fast-start' communities and regions would be identified at a number of sites in order to pilot schemes. Community health centres and comprehensive health organisation would be supported as structures promoting integration and co-ordination of delivery of services and the government would develop a continuum of services.

  In addition the Ministry of Health would be re-structured to reflect the new, broader approach to health.

- *Respecting the care provider.* A closer partnership for all care providers, the government and the general public was called for. Both paid and volunteer groups must be involved in planning health services.

  The restructuring of the health system would include plans to help care providers adjust to new circumstances, address abuse of providers, a safe working environment and pay equity. There would also be strengthened support for informal care providers as a vital aspect of bringing care closer to home.

- *Effective management of the new health system.* This depended on clear goals being defined at community, regional and provincial levels and managers taking ethically sound and financially responsible decisions on how to reach these goals. Accountable relationships at all levels must also be defined.

  There would be an increased emphasis on accountability by service providers to clients and taxpayers. The Provincial Health Council would publish an annual report and a 'report card' on the health of British Columbians. Professional legislation would be reviewed and amended where necessary to ensure consistency with principles regarding public protection, equity, due process and competency. Management and financial audits would be undertaken at all levels and new standards and protocols would be developed for the collection of information as well as the evaluation of outcomes.

The government recognised that the challenges presented by this reform were immense, but the changes would be made carefully, step by step in a flexible manner without losing sight of overall objectives. *New Directions for a Healthy British Columbia* was taken directly to the public through an extensive tour of almost every region in the province. The tour served as part of the government's commitment to consultation and open dialogue. Within the Ministry of Health detailed work plans which included provisions for consultative groups were completed for each of the priority actions. Work also proceeded on central projects such as the development of governance and funding structures and core services and standards.

To help local areas and communities assume responsibility for bringing health decision-making 'closer to home' six Executive Directors were appointed to work within the regions of the province. These directors held meetings with interest groups, elected officials, Ministry staff and the general public in an effort to keep consultation and involvement in the process as broadly based as possible. Community health planning groups were also established in all regions and several moved quickly forward to the setting up of Community Health Councils.

New Directions necessitated the introduction of legislation to set up a Provincial Health Council and Regional Health Authorities. The Council has a broad mandate to promote all aspects of the health of British Columbians and is a permanent body independent of government, charged with promoting public awareness and knowledge of health issues, developing a set of measurable provincial health goals and evaluating progress towards these goals. The Minister also established a broadly based advisory group consisting of major stakeholders in health care as well as groups of people who had not been well represented in the past in health planning, service and delivery.

Regional health authorities carry out regional planning and co-ordinate regional services. The board represents a coalition of communities within the region and consists of representatives of each Community Health Council and individuals appointed by the Minister.

Community Health Councils are the new local authority responsible for identifying local health priorities and co-ordinating and delivering health services. It is expected that in 1996 they will be composed of elected members and individuals appointed by the Minister. By spending carefully and shifting resources to meet needs the government of British Columbia hopes to keep pace with the changing requirements of citizens and keep health care affordable for all.

ALBERTA

Over the past several years expenditure on health services in Alberta has amounted to one-third of the total provincial government budget. This had begun to crowd out spending on other public services that can be equally important to health. The government recognised that whilst there was a need to maintain and even improve 'health' there was also a need to reduce expenditure and manage funds more effectively.[51] These needs were the impetus for the Rainbow Report[52] which in February 1990 presented the results of more than two years review , analysis and public consultation on the strengths and weaknesses of Alberta's health services. A constant theme of the representations made to the Commission was the need to restructure the health care system. In the Report, amongst 21 other recommendations made, was a call for legislation to ensure that the health of Albertans was consciously and publicly balanced with economic development and other initiatives. Individual responsibility was to be promoted and fostered through the establishment of local health authorities which had the power to make decisions and disburse funds relevant to the health of communities. Members would be locally elected and familiar with local priorities.

The structure envisaged by the Report included the setting up of regional authorities which would devise community care networks to assist consumers identify and assess health and health care information, programmes, services, facilities and treatment available. The government would assume an administrative role with responsibility for funding, co-ordinating and monitoring regional activities. The regional authority would take on the management of the health system within its health region. Thus the principle of community oriented care was foremost.

The Report also considered that regional health authorities should have the flexibility to engage more than one method of remuneration for provision. Fee-for-service, contract for service and salary were all reasonable forms of reimbursement and it was not necessary to have one particular system for all providers. This should provide different incentives to move the system towards provincial and regional goals and provide a better service for consumers.

On receipt of the Report the government established a task force of Ministers to undertake a review of the 21 recommendations made. The

---

51 *Report to Standing Policy Committee on Community Services* (Ministry of Health, 1993).
52 *Our Vision for Health* (The Premier's Commission on Future Health Care for Albertans, Edmonton, 1989).

review process included discussions with 'hundreds of individual Albertans and scores of interest groups'.[53] The results of the review and the government's response were published in *Partners in Health; the Governments Response to the Premier's Commission on Future Health Care for Albertans* some two years later. The government indicated that the health system would be oriented more towards home and community care in the future, with a more judicious use of new technology and greater use of information resources. There would be an emphasis on prevention and less need for treatment.

The health system would see more effective and co-operative use of all health professionals and fewer disciplinary boundaries, more attention to outcomes and less focus on input and activity. Funding systems would be based more on goals and accountability and less on historic precedent or volume of services.

In order to identify and respond to health priorities in communities and regions across the province the Minister appointed an Advisory Committee to initiate the development of health goals. The provincial government also endorsed a national plan to manage physician resources.

The Advisory Committee adopted a broad definition of health and identified nine health goals to:

- increase the number of years of good health by reducing illness;
- make decisions based on good information and research;
- include a health perspective in public policy;
- have appropriate, accessible and affordable health service;
- live in strong, supportive and healthy families and communities;
- live in a good physical environment;
- recognise and maximise individual potential in spite of biological differences;
- choose healthy behaviours;
- develop and maintain skills for facing the challenges of life in a healthy way.

These nine goals were scrutinised and responded to by other government departments and a wide range of health organisations in the community. Working groups also proposed health targets for four age groups; infants/children, adolescents, adults and older adults,

---

53 *Alberta Health Annual Report* (1991–92) p 5.

which were added to the agenda for discussion. The result of these deliberations was *Healthy Albertans in a Healthy Alberta*[54] which formed the basis of a series of Round Table consultations.

The mission of Alberta Health was stated to be:

To promote, maintain and improve the health of Albertans by providing direction in the management of resources, to ensure appropriate, accessible and affordable health services in the province.[55]

The major directions and challenges put to the Round Table sessions were addressed through several initiatives. First the health goals initiative provided the overall framework for identifying factors affecting Albertan health and setting priorities for targeting resources. The second area of major activity was a review of the funding and payment systems and how these affected delivery of services. Greater use of day surgery, outpatient services and community programmes were encouraged along with collaborative initiatives between institutional and community projects through special funding arrangements. Third, health promotion and community based care was promoted through an enhanced role for environmental health, expansion of home care and other strategies. The fourth area of work was that of health information, research and evaluation, so that health policy could be made on as sound an evidential basis as possible. Knowledge about the impact of reimbursement, organisation and delivery of services on access and quality was extremely limited so that management information systems would be set up and a Provincial Advisory Committee on Health Research established with government funding. Fifth, health human resources accounted for 70% of programme costs and 8% of the total workforce of Alberta. Sixth, a number of initiatives were introduced regarding health service re-organisation. There was concern that there was duplication, overlap and uncoordinated planning in the Albertan health system. The roles of all the sectors; hospitals, long term care facilities, health units and mental health services were examined and involved in a province wide consultation process. There appeared to be considerable support for local and regional planning and the need to develop innovative ways to deliver services. The Ministry of Health made it clear that no one model for planning was expected to work around the province, approaches needed to be flexible.

The final area for departmental work was that of effective communication with the public and with stakeholders. Changes could not occur without an understanding of the issues and a part in

---

54   Edmonton (1993).

55   *ibid.*

considering options by the public. This would require extensive consultation which would be a key focus of Round Table consultations.

The emphasis at Round Table discussions was clearly on the responsiveness of the system to consumer needs at different times in their lives. It was concluded that it was essential that health organisation was restructured to be flexible and capable of responding to different conditions. Imposition of a top-down system was not seen as likely to be sensitive to specific needs.[56]

As a consequence the Regional Health Authorities Act (1994) was the first legislative step taken in the restructuring of the system. It authorised the establishment of teams to manage the new health system as outlined in the three year business plan. The reformed health service is described as a 'consumer-driven system based on community priorities to form the cornerstone of future health services which will be delivered co-operatively by health providers and community organisations'.[57] Under the Act determination of needs and funding decisions will fall on the Authority rather than hospitals as had previously been the case. However this arrangement provides numerous opportunities for the provincial government to exercise its influence over the provision of health services and the type of services offered could from now on be regulated extensively.

CONCLUSION

It would be unfair to give the impression that health care reforms are being achieved smoothly in Canada and that all is 'sweetness and light' in the relationship between citizens and the executive. As elsewhere the reforms are driven by the escalating costs of medical inflation and in Canada's case progressive reductions in federal funding. Change is never easy and there has been some intransigence and reluctance on the part of public servants in the provincial Ministries of Health to embrace the recommendations made by independent bodies. Obviously where costs are of paramount concern there is a requirement to ensure that financial issues are under control and a tendency to keep a 'tight rein on the on the purse strings'. But in some cases the desire to keep hold of and to tighten those reins has extended to attempts to take too much control over policy and information.

In Nova Scotia, which is again typical, obtaining information from the Ministry of Health, which the Provincial Health Council regarded

---

56 *Our Bill of Health – Summary of Alberta Roundtables on Health* (November 1993).
57 Press Release 105–1994.

as essential to fulfil its role, was not always easy or even possible.[58] Much of the information that was withheld pertained to the comparative cost effectiveness of different policies and the impact of budget constraints. The Council considered there were several reasons for the difficulty. First, government agencies did not always place sufficient emphasis on providing the public with access to information. Second, despite the Freedom of Information Act some information was considered as privileged. The policy of the Provincial Health Council itself is that any information the Council has is openly available to the public on request.[59] The Ministry of Health would be unlikely in that case to release to the Council anything that might prove 'politically' embarrassing or sensitive. Finally, some of the health information requested by the Provincial Health Council was not routinely collected or reported by government.

To assess the appropriateness of funding for health services the Council needs detailed and comparative information. The effectiveness of consultation and public input is reduced considerably and the balance of power altered, when subject to incomplete information. The 'coyness' of the Ministry of Health seems inappropriate and unwarranted, given the spirit and overall thrust of health care reform in the province.

Nevertheless it is evident that Canada has been and is far more willing to open up the process of health service reforms and policy than is the case in either the UK or New Zealand. Health organisations have also been prepared to develop strategies and to make a concerted effort to counter government proposals where deemed necessary and to tackle intransigence with well informed arguments. In addition the emphasis on new public management seems not to have affected Canadian provincial government to the same extent. The possible reasons for this and the differences in constitutional underpinnings are explored in a later chapter, after analysis of the health reforms of New Zealand and the UK.

---

58 Nova Scotia Provincial Health Council, *Annual Report* (31 March 1993–94; 1994).

59 Information from the Provincial Health Council is free, easy to read and also available on audio-cassette and computer disk.

CHAPTER 3

NEW ZEALAND HEALTH SERVICES

INTRODUCTION

The New Zealand health services serve a much smaller population than that of either the UK or Canada. The population of some three and a half million is equivalent to, or smaller than, the size of many cities in other countries and is spread unevenly throughout an island country similar in size to the UK. There is therefore, not only considerable need to ensure fair and appropriate means of access to health services, but also a need to avoid duplication and under use of services, particularly in the highly specialised, technical fields of medicine which are renowned for being expenditure 'hungry'. In hard economic terms New Zealand's health spending as a percentage of Gross Domestic Product (GDP) has been consistently below average.[1] Though this level of expenditure is only slightly lower than that of the UK, it is considerably less than that spent on health in Canada.

The changes in the organisation of the health service in New Zealand, like those in the UK, have to be seen in the context of the general changes that have occurred in the nature of public service and government functions over the last 10 to 15 years. Again, as in the UK, the implementation of the reforms in New Zealand has been accompanied by controversy and criticism.

From the mid-1930s through to the 1960s New Zealand's health services expanded rapidly and resources tended to increase accordingly. As in the UK and Canada universal entitlement stood as a 'symbol of altruism and richness of public spirit'[2] and the idea of health care as a social responsibility was deeply rooted in people's minds. New Zealand took pride in its state funded health care system and publicly funded hospitals. But during those years little consideration appeared to have been given to the realities of a rapidly expanding system and the implications of a continual escalation of public expenditure. There was a fragmentation of funding and a lack of integration and co-ordination in overall provision which failed to provide a cost effective service. Unlike Canada, New Zealand failed to

---

1   In 1993 New Zealand spent 7.6% of its GDP on health compared to an OECD average of 8.2%; OECD provisional data.

2   C Flood and M Trebilcock,'Voice and Exit in New Zealand's Health Care Sector' (1994) in *Contracting in the Health Sector* (Legal Research Foundation, Auckland University).

control user charges, particularly for general practitioner services, which were prohibitive for some socio-economic groups and contributed to unequal access to care and greater consumption of secondary provision.[3] Equality of access was also reduced by the growth in private insurance and private health provision for those who could afford it.

During the next decade a series of Royal Commissions reported on the possible means of achieving greater accountability for public financing[4] and an initially shelved White Paper in 1974 proposed that 14 Regional Health Authorities (RHAs) should be responsible for the delivery of a comprehensive health service constituting primary, hospital, rehabilitation and public health provision, and that the state should contract with voluntary agencies to facilitate fully integrated health services.[5]

However, a change of government led to the establishment of a Special Advisory Committee on Health Service Organisation and a revamping of the previously dormant White Paper. Subsequent changes made under the Area Health Boards Act (1983) introduced population based funding and enabled hospital boards to move, on a voluntary basis, towards integrated area health boards. These were to 'promote and protect the health of the people in their area' by co-ordinating the public, private and voluntary sectors. To ensure an appropriate balance between public and personal health spending the 1983 Act required health boards to address public health as well as treatment services. Community participation was provided for at three levels: at the level of the elected board, service development groups and community committees.

Establishment of area health boards was incremental, very much dependent on the outcome of negotiations about amalgamation and boundaries. A period of service planning followed in which success was determined by the development of good communications in order to ensure both public community groups and professionals understood the changes and were involved in the debate and decision-making process. The process was only completed in 1989 when the additional developments in the New Zealand Health Charter, and the establishment of health goals and targets consolidated the area health board reforms and set a new direction for public health. But before the new structure could properly demonstrate its worth a different ethos; one generally associated with business and the private sector, began to

---

3   Davis, *Health and Health Care in New Zealand* (Auckland, 1981).

4   Royal Commission on State Services (1961–2) Royal Commission on Social Security (1969–72) Royal Commission of Inquiry into Hospital and Related Services (1971–73).

5   *A Health Service for New Zealand* (Wellington, 1974).

infiltrate the system. The New Zealand government asserted that the health system was failing to produce sufficient benefit for its cost, that problems of access remained and that it was evident that there was a lack of responsiveness to *consumer* needs.

THE RECENT REFORMS

Fundamental changes to the New Zealand health care system were announced in a Green and White Paper, *Your Health and the Public Health; a Statement of Government Health Policy* in July 1991.[6] The radical surgery suggested in that paper developed further the tenets of an earlier report published by the Gibbs Committee in 1988 which had conducted an extensive review of the New Zealand hospital system against the background of international developments in health economics and management of health care systems.[7]

The Gibbs Committee had found that the almost universally familiar difficulties experienced in New Zealand were indicative of serious deficiencies in the system. The tone and the recommendations of Gibbs sound very familiar to those who have followed the debates which have raged in relation to the National Health Service (NHS) in the UK. In fact, the observations of the UK NHS Management Inquiry Report[8] could largely be taken to refer to the New Zealand hospital system as perceived by the Gibbs Committee. Gibbs argued that the management structure of the New Zealand health service was over centralised, bureaucratic and confused. In contrast to the private sector there was a lack of management information, cost consciousness and productivity monitoring. Efficient management was hampered by the dual role of hospital boards as both funders and suppliers of services and there was scant evidence of business expertise and skills amongst elected board members. Furthermore, consumers had no way of directly determining the pattern of services supplied or of having their needs and wishes given priority.

Accordingly, the Gibbs taskforce recommended that although the government should remain the main hospital provider, purchaser and provider roles should be clearly separated and an element of modified competition introduced between hospitals. This limited market, it was argued, would facilitate a radical change in management, operating

---

6   S Upton (Wellington, 1991).

7   *Unshackling the Hospitals* (The Report of the Hospital and Related Services Taskforce, 1988).

8   (Griffiths, 1983).

principally through more vigilant monitoring of financial performance and the quality and quantity of what was produced.

Gibbs advised that the system be funded from central government, on a population basis, through a newly established National Health Commission to six Regional Health Authorities (RHAs). The RHAs would purchase services from hospitals and other providers on behalf of the people of their region. They would neither manage nor own any services but would contract with public, private and voluntary providers on a competitively neutral basis. The existing hospital and area health boards would amalgamate to form new entities which would be paid only for the services they provided.

RHAs would have responsibility to the consumer only, acting as an independent body with the 'power of the purse' to look after their interests. Consequently they would have none of the conflict of interests experienced by the hospital and area health boards. Choice of health care services would be influenced by RHA resources, the demographic characteristics of the region, the views of health professionals and more particularly by the people who used the services. Another important function of the RHA would be to enable a cap or limit to be placed on total public funding. The Gibbs taskforce believed that resulting efficiency gains would reduce waiting lists and release incentives in the system which would in turn encourage more services to be offered by providers.

Gibbs recognised that placing a limit on expenditure would require priorities to be set by RHAs. But as elected bodies RHAs would be in a position to be concerned with the interests of the consumer in their region. In their contracts they would specify the quantity and quality of services and they would monitor provider performance. Amalgamated hospital and area health boards would function in a similar way to public companies and concentrate on running efficient services.

What eventually emerged in the Upton Report and subsequent legislation encompassed some quite fundamental differences from those recommended by the Gibbs Committee and put New Zealand's health system on a totally new footing. The reforms have four main stated aims:

- to ensure everyone has access to *an agreed core of services*;

- to improve the heath status of the community;

- to achieve better value for money and greater accountability for expenditure;

- to manage the *financial liability of the government* in an area under increasing pressure.

It appears clear from these aims that the main focus of the reforms is the curbing of public expenditure on health by limitation of public provision to core services.

In order to forward these aims the health care structure of New Zealand has been altered considerably under the Health and Disability Services Act (1993), although, as in the UK, many of the reforms were in the process of being put into effect before the Act actually came into force. Much stems from the separation of the purchasing role from the provider role and the attempt to integrate funding for a comprehensive range of health services and disability services.

Area health boards, which had been predominately locally elected and which had previously carried out both purchasing and provider functions, were abolished and replaced by four RHAs, which now carry out the purchasing function and 23 Crown Health Enterprises (CHE) which provide the bulk of services.

The abolition of the elected area health boards was regarded in many quarters as being an 'extraordinary political act'.[9] It reversed not only the government's election policy but fundamentally changed the way in which the health care had been administered *without any public discussion*. Whilst recognising that their operation was not beyond reproach, area health boards were still evolving their relationship with management and with central government, in addition to grappling with the difficult issues arising from medical inflation. Their abolition was seen as a diminution of local participation in decision-making, reducing not only the sense of ownership reflected in community support for health facilities and services but also the checks and balances necessary to counteract domination by central government. Area health boards had also shared regional council boundaries, facilitating the communitarian values embedded in the Local Government Act (1974). It was thus argued that democratic values had been replaced by a concept of economic rationalism.

The four RHAs, the Northern RHA in Auckland, the Midland RHA in Hamilton, the Central RHA in Wellington and the Southern RHA in Dunedin, which have taken on the purchasing role, are independent Crown agencies with populations of somewhat differing overall characteristics. For example, Southern region has a relatively older population, Midland proportionally more young people, and Northern region includes a number of significant ethnic groups.[10] The three

9   Martin J, 'The case for a local voice' (1992) in *Health Reforms: a Second Opinion* (Wellington Health Action Committee).

10 *Purchasing for your Health; a performance report on the first year of the Regional Health Authorities and the Public Health Commission* (Performance Monitoring and Review Unit, Ministry of Health, 1993–1994).

primary functions of RHAs are to assess the needs for health and disability services, to purchases services accordingly and to monitor provider performance against purchase agreements. RHAs buy services for the residents in their respective areas based on the health care requirements of the region and are responsible for deciding the level of purchases they will make within each service category. Their purchasing decisions must be compatible with policy guidelines issued by the Minister of Health.

The scope of services purchased is extensive and covers primary, secondary and tertiary care, including accident and sickness provision, nursing home care and residential and domiciliary services for the elderly and physically disabled and those with learning difficulties. The integration of accident, sickness and disability support purchasing was perceived as an opportunity to provide more effective and flexible services through a capacity to switch resources between health and social care, according to local requirements. However, financial provision is divided into two parts, one for personal health services and one for disability support services. This 'ring fencing' was designed to ensure that no transfer of funding takes place between the two main service areas without parliamentary approval.

RHAs did not at first have responsibility for purchasing public health services which accounts for a relatively small, though not insignificant, part of health expenditure. Responsibility for public health was kept separate from the trend towards integration and was initially the function of a newly established Public Health Commission.[11] However this body quite rapidly met its demise, becoming subsumed within the Ministry of Health. Responsibility for the purchase of the majority of public health services has now passed to the Regions for both regional and some national requirements.

Section 10 of the Health and Disability Support Services Act (1993) provides that every RHA shall strive:

(a) to promote personal health;

(b) to promote the care and support for, and autonomy of people with disabilities; and

(c) to meet the Crown's social and other objectives with regard to personal health services in accordance with, and to the extent enabled by, its funding agreement.

The four RHAs may purchase services from a range of public, private or voluntary providers. They are expected to have detailed knowledge of the health needs and preferences of the region and of providers able to offer services. The focus is on buying the best quality care from any

---

11   Discussed at pp 89–90.

source at the best price. RHAs set the quality and standards of provision which providers are expected to meet through contracts and are responsible for the monitoring of the delivery of these. They receive their finance from central government through an agreement on health priorities. Funding is based on the size and characteristics of the community served and is thus allocated on an age adjusted equitable formula with a small special needs component for socio-economic factors.

It was intended in the reforms that RHAs would be independent purchasers of health services accountable to, but operating at 'arms length' from central government. RHAs are to promote neither their own nor any other institutional interests to the detriment of the best interests of their resident population. However the degree of independence of RHAs is open to debate.

First, each RHA has a board of up to seven members who are not elected, as was the case with Area Health Boards, but are appointed by the Minister of Health for a term of not more than three years, although reappointment is permitted.[12] Flood and Trebilcock point out that appointment rather than election, plus the fact that the RHA board determines its members salaries[13] provides an incentive, with a view to reappointment or some other public sector job opportunities, not to make decisions contrary to government policy.[14]

Second, s 25 of the Health and Disability Services Act empowers the Minister of Health to issue such directions as the Minister considers necessary or expedient in any matter relating to the RHA. Before doing so however there is an obligation on the Minster to consult with the RHA concerned and the direction must be published in the *Gazette* and laid before Parliament as soon as is practicable. This requirement at least promotes openness if only in terms of formal provisions.

Third, and possibly most importantly section 8 of the Health and Disabilities Act (1993) provides that prior to entering into a funding agreement the Minister of Health must give written notice of the Crown's objectives in relation to:

- the health status of the communities served by the purchaser;
- the health services or the disability services, or both, to be purchased;
- the terms of access to those services and the assessment and review procedures to be used in determining access to those services or such of those services as are specified in the notice;
- the standard of those services;

---

12 Section 35(2) and the Second Schedule of the Health and Disabilities Services Act (1993).

13 Up to a maximum set by the Minister of Health.

14 see *supra* (note 2) p 67.

- the special needs of Maori and other particular communities or people for those services.

The notice, given in the form of policy guidelines, must be published and laid before Parliament. The primary task of policy guidelines is stated to be the provision of help to RHAs to develop their annual Purchase Plans and Statements of Intent, which provide Parliament with information on the purchasing intentions of RHAs each year, and to aid the development of medium term strategic plans. Policy guidelines have no legal effect and give no rights to third parties, but set out:

- the governments priorities for publicly funded health and disability support services;

- the services which RHAs are required to purchase for the population of their regions;

- the way in which RHAs are to go about purchasing these services;

- the mechanisms to hold RHAs to account for meeting their objectives.

The New Zealand government regards two elements as critical for the successful purchase of goods and services; purchases must meet defined needs and must represent value for money. These are laudable aims, but in practice RHAs are agencies of government rather than independent entities. Government first decides what it wants to purchase and then communicates this to the purchasing agency. In determining which health and disability support services are to be purchased, the Ministry of Health seeks advice from a wide range of institutions and consults with a number of organisations including the four RHAs, the Core Services Committee, other government agencies such as Te Puni Kokiri, the Ministry of Womens Affairs, the Department of Social Welfare, the Ministry of Pacific Island Affairs and the Accident Rehabilitation and Compensation Insurance Corporation, as well as other health and disability sector groups. This advice is incorporated into the Ministry of Health's own analysis of requirements and advice to the Minister of Heath, who then presents the draft guidelines to Cabinet.

Government policy is translated into RHA purchasing requirements through service obligations, which are set out in the policy guidelines document and which comprise three elements; the range of health and disability support services, minimum coverage and/or terms of access, and minimum standards of safety and quality.[15] The level of description of requirements setting out services obligations is intended

---

15 Shipley, *Policy Guidelines for Regional Health Authorities* (1995/96) Annex 1 pp 48–77.

to be broad enough to allow RHAs flexibility to purchase services in ways that meet the particular needs of their populations.[16] But one must question whether this actually is the case when the organisational structure and financial constraints are taken together. However, policy guidelines are intended to be more than a shopping list of health and disability support services.

They also describe the principles on which the government wishes its agencies to base their purchase decisions and the areas in which the government wishes to see health gains.[17]

The principles referred to are equity, effectiveness, efficiency, safety, acceptability and risk management. A package which might be considered as something of a tall order.

One of the key functions of the policy guidelines is to provide the basis for the Funding Agreement between the Minister of Health and each RHA. The Funding Agreement is the vehicle of RHA activity and sets out the expectations and the conditions under which RHAs will operate during the coming year.[18] It is in effect the accountability document between the Minister of Health and health service purchasers, and is strictly confidential between the parties so as not to confer any negotiating advantage on providers. It indicates proposed levels of services, financial budgets and the restrictions under which purchasers operate and is signed at the beginning of the financial year, when purchasers are also required to have their Statements of Intent tabled before Parliament within 12 sitting days of receipt by the Minister. These statements are consistent with the more technical and detailed Funding Agreements and form the basis of purchasers accountability to Parliament.

RHA objectives[19] are to meet those of the Government set out in the policy guidelines under s 8 of the Health and Disabilities Act (1993). However there is an important exception to RHA objectives in that they are required only to meet Crown objectives and those of their own set out under s 10 in so far as their funding agreement permits them to do so. One commentator has pointed to the possibility of divergence between the *publicly notified* objectives under s 8 and the necessity of the *confidentiality* of the Funding Agreement.

A more cynical observer might come to the conclusion that this represents a means for the Crown to present an optimal public image

---

16   *ibid* p 18.
17   *ibid* p 48.
18   Section 21 Health and Disability Services Act.
19   Section 10.

whilst achieving a less publicly palatable agenda through the means of the confidential funding agreement.[20]

DISABILITY SUPPORT SERVICES

Prior to the reforms, responsibility for disability support services in New Zealand was divided between several government agencies. Consequently funding arrangements were divided and somewhat complicated. Some services were financed on a demand-driven basis which made expenditure difficult to control and offered little incentive for resources to be used efficiently and effectively. Other services operated on a fixed budget which meant that once their financial allocation had been depleted no services could be provided. Those agencies who both funded and delivered services protected their own institution and rarely sought provision from other organisations even if their own were not the most appropriate, cost effective options to meet people's needs. In addition funding was generally locked into institutional and hospital care and was not available for those wishing to remain in their own home or community.

As a result it was difficult for those with disabilities to be certain which agency they should approach to deal with their needs and it was not unknown for some people to be shunted from one agency to another. A person's primary disability determined which agency took responsibility for funding and providing their services. There was sometimes a failure to determine total needs or where other needs were considered they tended to be minimised. Consequently, those with disabilities were often placed in a 'take it or leave it' situation; faced with a choice between accepting inappropriate services or having no services at all.

Changes to this unsatisfactory framework began some time before the reforms to the health system. A consultation document *Support for Independence* explored possible solutions to the problems and culminated in a government policy statement issued in 1992 entitled *Support for Independence: A New Deal*. There would be a purchaser/ provider split, agencies providing services would be separate from those responsible for funding them and all funding for one type of service would be located in one agency. To ensure that money intended for disability support services would not be spent on any other services the funding for disability support services would be 'ring-fenced' from any other controlled by purchasers. The single agency responsible for

---

20   C Rowling, 'The Contracting Process-Building New Relationships in Health Care' (1994) in
     Contracting in the Health Sector see *supra* (note 2).

purchasing disability support services would be given an integrated budget; a combination of fixed and demand driven funds, in an attempt to overcome previous expenditure shortcomings.

Before deciding which agency would have responsibility for purchasing disability support services the New Zealand government carried out a consultation exercise. Two options were presented, the Department of Social Welfare, which had previously been the major 'purchaser' of community based disability support services, or the newly established RHAs. A series of regional seminars were held to inform the public and interested organisations of the issues.

The main issues were the requisite characteristics of a disability support services purchasing agency, the potential problems associated with the main contenders and how these could best be resolved. Over 400 submissions were received and from these the main characteristics required of a purchasing agency were identified as:

- an understanding, positive attitude towards people with disabilities;

- a commitment to consumer empowerment;

- accountability to consumers;

- flexibility and innovation;

- a concern with the integration and co-ordination of services.

Opinion was divided however on whether the Department of Social Welfare or RHAs could fulfil these requirements and act as purchaser. In the event, the task was given to the RHAs and the Ministry of Health was to provide policy advice to government on disability support services as well as personal health matters.

The process of transfer of responsibility to RHAs began in 1993 and was expected to be completed by the beginning of the financial year 1995.[21] Providers of disability support services are varied, ranging from the Crown Health Enterprises, which provide a range of hospital and community services, to non-profit organisations such as charitable trusts, church based agencies and incorporated societies of varying sizes, and profit making businesses such as rest homes and private hospitals.

The new framework, as stated by the New Zealand government, is designed to ensure a focus on the consumer, to reduce duplication, clarify responsibility and ensure accountability. A high level of consumer participation in the development of disability support services, effective appeal and grievance procedures which involve an

---

21   The financial year in New Zealand runs form 1 July to 30 June.

independent appeals authority and consistent standards of assessment have also been promised.

It has been recognised that in the past assessment processes were often used to test whether a person was eligible for a service, rather than identify their needs and the services to meet them. It is hoped that by separating service assessment and service co-ordination from service provision it will be possible to find the package of services which best meets need. Two government publications, *Standards for Needs Assessment for People with Disabilities* and *Guidelines for Service Co-ordination* require the separation of assessment, co-ordination and provision to be clearly defined. However, they will not necessarily be carried out by different organisations and RHAs have been made responsible for implementing monitoring procedures to ensure that any potential conflicts of interest between assessment, service co-ordination and provision do not occur in practice.

Assessment services have been given three years to meet the Standards which were developed in conjunction with the disability community.[22] From 1 July 1997 RHAs will be required to purchase needs assessments only from services which comply with these Standards. Briefly, the Standards require entry to the assessment service to be easy, both procedurally and physically. The service is to have written policies which are followed by all staff, and information is to be provided to the person being assessed in an appropriate form. The outcome of assessment is to be an accurate identification of *individual* needs and must be culturally appropriate. People being assessed must be treated at all times with dignity and respect.

Guidelines on service co-ordination are also available.[23] Service co-ordination identifies the package of services required to meet a person's needs and will also determine which of those needs can be met by publicly funded services as well as explore other options for addressing any other needs. Consequently, comprehensive knowledge of the range of services available in the region, communication and negotiation ability and capacity are essential.

In terms of provision RHAs purchase a range of services, depending on national and community priorities, relating to assessment and social assistance. This includes information, advocacy, counselling, supervision and companionship services, personal care, domestic assistance, equipment, residential and hospital care, rehabilitation services such as occupational and speech therapy and life

---

22 *Standards or Needs Assessments for People with Disabilities* (1994).

23 *Guidelines for Service Co-ordination* (1994).

skills training, respite care and relief for carers and behavioural support and treatment services.

Other programmes established under the Disabled Person's Community Welfare Act (1975) and functions of the Community Funding Agency which is concerned with vocational services for people with disabilities are currently in the process of being transferred to RHAs. Ways in which the disability support and special education systems can work together are also being considered.

Despite government reassurances the changes to disability support services and the rework of the 1975 Act have been criticised for linking health and disability together. Historically, that linkage has led to a secondary status for those with disabilities and implies dependency. There is also concern that assessment for services will be overly subject to financial considerations and made primarily on medical criteria, pulling disabilities back onto the 'medical model roundabout' which is regarded by many as inappropriate.[24]

PRIMARY CARE

Primary health care is concerned with personal health services to which people have direct access and refers in the main to general practitioner services which have been paid for traditionally in New Zealand on a 'fee for service' basis. General practitioners influence expenditure in two ways; by referring patients to other services such as laboratory tests, prescribing pharmaceuticals or for specialist consultations and through the payments they receive for providing care (known as general medical subsidies (GMS)). Purchasers, previously the Department of Health but now RHAs, pay the GP a subsidy, for those patients eligible, for each consultation. The level of GMS varies according to the age of the patient and their eligibility for community service cards and high use health cards. GPs are permitted to charge patients as well as claim the subsidy.

Because of the 'demand driven' nature by which most primary health care services are currently purchased RHAs can meet major financial difficulties. High levels of service can mean that RHAs face additional expense irrespective of the need for, or effectiveness of, service provision. Consequently, all RHAs are now piloting capitation contracts as a means of managing GP reimbursement. Under this scheme the revenue of GPs is based on the number of patients in their

---

24 W Wicks, 'Implications for those with Disabilities' (1992) in *Health Reforms: a Second Opinion* (Wellington Health Action Committee).

care, rather than the number of times they see their patients. Through this approach the government points out that GP's gain surety of income and RHAs are not exposed to additional expenditure if GPs see more patients more often than expected. In addition, capitation is thought to encourage service delivery by the most appropriate health professional, as GPs are not required to deliver all services themselves.

Incentives have thus moved from encouraging the maximum number of services to promotion of the enrolment of a maximum number of patients. Currently RHAS have only limited capability to verify patient enrolment but are keen to see patient registration introduced. At the same time however they must recognise the need for patient choice. Midland Health for example are proposing a scheme of voluntary registration and enrolment by suggesting that users register with a family health professional or group of professionals for a particular range of services. Initially registration will focus on general practice, or maternity services or child health. But as family health teams develop people will be able to register increasingly with a team of their choice.[25] Midland Health emphasise that registration with one team would not exclude the possibility of consulting another health professional if desired. Over time it is envisaged that family health teams will come to form part of a larger integrated care organisation which will provide a network of family health teams, hospital and specialist services. Whilst the benefits of integrated health care can be immense, they may potentially curtail user choice. Integrative care organisations might also be seen as the ideal structure to facilitate the introduction of health care plans or the wholesale privatisation of the health system

It is not only the GMS that causes financial problems for the fixed budget RHA's. Whilst the GMS has been growing at a rate similar to inflation, expenditure on referred services such as pharmaceutic and diagnostic tests has grown at over 10% per annum. To try to curb this RHAs have introduced a number of 'pilot' budget holding contracts by which GPs are given nominal budgets for pharmaceutic and diagnostic tests. Any savings made are shared between the RHA and the GP practice on the proviso that savings are spent on additional services.[26] Risk of over expenditure is held by the RHA. This means that GPs are not prohibited from ordering additional services over and above the budget if there is a clinical need.

RHAs have also contracted with the Preferred Medicine Centre (PreMeC), to encourage rational prescribing by GPs. PreMeC seeks to

---

25 *Have Your Say* (Midland Health, 1994).
26 *Purchasing for your health; a performance report of the first year* (1993/4).

inform GPs of the best prescribing practice. Enrolment varies from 74-94% across regions and there is some evidence that cheaper but equally efficacious treatments are actually being prescribed.[27]

From the users perspective, the value of the General Medical Services Benefit has fallen considerably since it was introduced, from around 75% of the total fee to less than 20%.[28] At the same time as the structural changes were made the New Zealand government abolished subsidised general practitioner visits for many patients, increased pharmaceutical charges and introduced partial user charges for care received in public hospitals. Due to public outcry this latter innovation was abandoned, but targeted subsidies and user charges for general practitioners and pharmaceuticals survived. In order to avoid paying the highest rate of user charges for these services 'low and modest income earners' must now present an entitlement card called the *Community Services Card*. Flood and Trebilcock argue that this increases neither the efficiency nor the fairness of the system.

They point out that although user charges may seem justifiable in economic terms, in that they should operate as a rationing mechanism, restricting patient demand to those services they value most; in reality very few patients actually abuse the system or enjoy consuming unneeded health services. In general only those services advocated by a general practitioner are taken up. They argue that what is really needed is an incentive for third party payers to choose the most cost effective treatments. That is currently not the present case, instead the imposition of user charges merely passes on costs to third party payers whether this be the state or a private insurance company.

CONSULTATION

It goes without saying that communities have a legitimate interest in the nature and shape of the publicly funded health and disability service. Consultation provisions were strengthened to some extent after criticism of requirements in the Health and Disability Services Bill. There is a statutory requirement that RHAs and other purchasers consult both users and providers of services in its region on a regular basis.[29] In addition to the statutory requirements the policy guidelines state that RHAs have a responsibility to ensure that the communities they are consulting are provided with adequate information on both relevant issues and their complexity before being asked for their view.

---

27   *ibid* p 123.
28   Flood and Trebilcock *supra* (note 2) p 14.
29   Section 34 Health and Disability Services Act (1993).

RHAs also have an obligation to provide feedback at the end of the consultation period. Policy guidelines also state that consultation processes play an integral part in the monitoring of RHAs by the Ministry. RHAs are expected to outline in their Purchase Plans how they intend to develop their communication and consultation strategies, disseminate information and monitor strategies to ensure they are effective. Consequently, as a minimum RHAs are expected to develop consultation strategies which:

- identify the issues and outline the basis on which the issues were identified;

- identify the relevant communities and other important players involved;

- devise a time frame for consultation, allowing for sufficient debate and input from the community;

- attend to Maori interests, taking account of the Crowns obligation under the Treaty of Waitangi, by giving particular attention in the Purchase Plan to consultation and the three-year strategy for improving Maori health and by acknowledging ownership of the information imparted;

- consider the results of consultation carefully, inform participants of the outcome and *give reasons for accepting or rejecting some views*.[30]

To date, RHAs have generally produced some comprehensive consultation documents and sought comments on their purchasing intentions for the next financial year. For example, Southern Region produced a clear Draft Purchase Plan for 1995/6 which included a list of community liaison contacts and head office contact numbers and invited submissions from the public. This followed on from an earlier publication *Planning for the South* which outlined Southern's long-term strategy for the distribution of services in the region and marked the beginning of the consultation process. Once submissions had closed on the draft plan the Southern Region published a summary of them along with responses from the Authority.

Midland Health set out their proposals for the forthcoming financial year in a consultation document *Have Your Say*,[31] which included a cut out page and Freepost address for the return of comments. Copies of the booklet were mailed to individuals who had expressed an interest and were made available in libraries and other

---

30 *Policy Guidelines for Regional Health Authorities* (Shipley, 1995/96).

31 See *supra* (note 25).

community places throughout the region. Meetings were also held at major locations and Midland state that they advertise their willingness to hold meetings with any groups who specifically request it.[32] Midland have also listed other available documents and set up toll-free phone numbers for users to contact Community Relations Managers.

Whether these quite extensive consultation processes will continue remains to be seen. Northern Health have indicated that they have now 'made a strategic move toward consulting only if and when necessary'. This means that consultation will be commissioned only when a major or material change is sought in service provision.[33] Northern seem to intend in future to rely more on encouraging providers, through contract specification, to build up consultation and review processes with communities and to themselves concentrate more on gathering demographic and epidemiological information, rather than ascertaining directly the views of service users. Whether this will meet with legislative requirements and be acceptable to the Ministry of Health under policy guidelines remains to be seen.

In evaluating RHA consultation processes the Ministry states that it will also refer to the principles outlined in a number of other government documents which give guidance on consultation requirements in other areas of public policy. There are also a number of instances where RHAs are specifically required to inform the Minister of their consultation processes. These relate generally to material changes in the provision of services which might significantly affect either providers or users of services.

The Performance Monitoring and Review Unit has reported that communities are beginning to receive services provided in a way they consider more appropriate as a result of the consultation exercises with providers and communities already carried out by RHAs.[34] However, the question has been raised whether sufficient credence would ever be given to the outcome of consultation to displace, in practice, obligations set out in RHA Funding Agreements with the Crown. Where RHAs have failed to give due consideration to the results of public consultation exercises which have not conflicted with either their respective Funding Agreement or with Crown objectives an action in administrative law would probably lie.[35] But where there is conflict, Rowling points out that recent experience of consultation

---

32   Letter from Midland Health Community Communications Manager (April 1995).

33   Letter from Northern Health Services Quality Manager (April 1995).

34   *Purchasing for Health; a performance report on the first year* (Ministry of Health, 1993–4).

35   See J McGechan; *Air New Zealand Limited v Wellington International Airport Limited* (HC Wellington Registry, 1992 CP No 403/91), which is taken into account in Ministry evaluations of RHA consultation processes.

carried out in respect of the corporatisation of the electricity industry demonstrates the potential difficulty of challenging any RHA decision on this basis. So long as the RHA has not predetermined the matter and can clearly demonstrate that it considered the results of consultation, there is no imperative to implement those results. Consequently he argues that it seems likely that the consultation process will probably be more of a forum for gathering information and airing views rather than a catalyst for any meaningful change to RHA policy, particularly when the serious financial constraints placed on RHAs are also taken into account.[36]

It is worth mentioning here that the Accident Rehabilitation and Compensation Insurance Corporation (ACC) also purchases health care services. The ACC is charged with the administration of New Zealand's accident rehabilitation scheme and funds services for those who have to use the health care system as a result of an accident. This takes place through two primary means; subsidies for GP fees, physiotherapy fees and the like and reimbursement to the Crown. The latter covers funding to RHAs for accident services which are currently paid for by RHAs. These services are not explicitly contracted for by RHAs but form part of their global contracts with providers. In 1992 the government agreed that RHAs would assume responsibility for integrated accident and illness health care purchasing, subject to a number of constraints.

This responsibility includes continuing the purchase of services currently funded through Crown payments to RHAs and the eventual transfer of purchasing responsibility for each service wherever possible. However, the ACC has retained the right to purchase health services directly in a residual manner if this is deemed appropriate or necessary and is agreed by the relevant Minister. Where a service may not be initially regarded as readily transferable RHAs are expected to work with the ACC to develop suitable trials and pilots to examine the issues and test the feasibility of each potential transfer, within the limits of resources available. Further work is occurring on purchase agreements for accident services and RHAs are to be consulted in the policy development process.[37]

Monitoring is also an integral part of the RHA operational cycle. RHAs monitor providers to ensure they are receiving the levels and quality of service demanded by purchase agreements. Purchasers report to the Ministry of Health on a quarterly basis on all aspects of performance and on a monthly basis with financial information. The

---

36   C Rowling see *supra* (note 2) p 52.
37   *Policy Guidelines for RHAs* (Shipley, 1995/6) p 24.

Ministry monitors purchasers to ensure that the requirements of the funding agreement have been met, to identify areas that require future policy development, to highlight comparative performance and create incentives for good performance. Purchasers are also required to report publicly against their Statements of Intent within three months of the year end. This is in the form of an Annual Report which is tabled before Parliament.

CROWN HEALTH ENTERPRISES

Major public hospitals are run under the control of organisations known as Crown Health Enterprises (CHEs). Although these are not regarded as the only institutional form appropriate for publicly owned facilities they currently provide the bulk of provision. CHEs are owned by the government on behalf of citizens and are synonymous with State Owned Enterprises in other public service sectors. Significantly, New Zealand has continued the purchaser/provider split through to ministerial level and created a new Crown Health ministerial portfolio for provider organisations. There are two shareholding ministers, the Minister of Finance and the Minister of Crown Health Enterprises, to whom the directors of CHE boards are accountable.

To assist the initial development of CHEs, the government established an advisory committee for each of the former 14 area health boards through the National Interim Provider Board (NIPB), which was set up in 1991 to make recommendations on the restructuring of the health care system within the principles laid down by government.[38] Each committee undertook a configuration study to determine the number and organisation of CHEs emerging from its area health board and evolved a plan for the establishment for each CHE. The time allocated for this process was only six months. In the event some 23 CHEs emerged from the existing area health boards.

CHEs are expected to operate in a competitively neutral environment in which public hospitals have no advantage over other alternative suppliers. Thus, CHEs are expected to gain contracts through the efficient delivery of good quality health services. Section 25 of the Crown Health Services Act (1993) provides that:

> the principal objective of every Crown Health Enterprise shall be to operate as a successful business that provides health services and disability services, or both, and that assists in meeting the Crown's social objectives by providing such services in accordance with its

---

38 *Providing Better Health Care for New Zealanders* (National Interim Provider Board, May 1992).

statement of intent and any purchase agreement entered into by it, and to this end, to be

(a) as profitable and efficient as comparable businesses that are not owned by the Crown; and

(b) an organisation that upholds the ethical standards generally expected of providers of such services; and

(c) a good employer; and

(d) an organisation that exhibits a sense of social responsibility by having regard to the interests of the community in which it operates.

The combination of running a profitable business, together with the maintenance of ethical standards and social objectives may present a potentially divergent set of objectives in the context of health. But, as Flood and Trebilcock comment, it may be that the government expects CHEs to operate as successful and efficient businesses only to a limited extent, given that they are expected also to fulfil the Crown's policy objectives set out under section 8 of the Health Services and Disability Support Act. In other words, the concept of a 'sufficient and successful business' is not that which is understood in the private sector.[39]

Although it was envisaged that there should be an 'arms length' relationship between government and the operational management of CHE's they are subject to a certain amount of political influence and are not free to operate autonomously. Not only are they accountable to government for their performance measured against targets set by the shareholding Ministers, but there are a number of legislative provisions which curb their operations as 'free marketeers'.

Unlike private providers, a CHE can be required to provide a particular service by the Minister of Health, although a reasonable price must be paid by the RHA.[40] Furthermore, s 51 of the Health and Disability Services Act confers considerable contracting power on RHAs, permitting them to force providers to contract on specified terms, where no alternative agreement between them can be secured. This provision is put into effect by an RHA issuing a notice of terms and conditions either individually or by way of public notice.[41] The s 51 mechanism might be seen as a spur to CHEs and other providers to take the negotiation and contracting process on board and glean as much knowledge as quickly as possible about the whole process. Whilst initially all contracts were for 'block' levels of services at fixed prices, RHAs are now moving to a greater level of specificity in

---

39 *Contracting in the Health Sector see supra* (note 2) p 35.

40 Section 40 Health Service and Disability Support Services Act (1993).

41 This mechanism was used for the roll over of services for the 1993/4 contract year for both CHEs and general practitioners, and remains in place for the latter until January 1996.

contracting so that CHEs need to develop negotiating skills in order to balance the level of risk which lay previously with them.

It was anticipated that the new management structure of state owned health care organisations would be able to provide scope for future development into more specialised units, so long as this would improve efficiency without encouraging inefficient, overprotected monopolies. In the future it is envisaged that CHEs will seek to form joint ventures, partnerships and alliances with other public and private providers and may wish to sub-contract medical or other services, if it is thought that this would be more efficient or less expensive.

However, current changes to health provisions are subject to the Commerce Act (1986), the aim of which is to promote competition in New Zealand markets.[42] Actions prohibited under the Act include arrangements between competitors which substantially lessen competition in the market or reduce the competitiveness of another, price fixing, and the use of a dominant position in the market to prevent competition. Previous restrictions on the treatment of private patients in public funded organisations also no longer apply, so that CHEs may now treat patients who are funded privately.

There are also a number of other potential difficulties for CHEs arising from the pro-competitive and regulatory structure. In order to be able to plan effectively CHEs need a degree of certainty about funding levels which enables them to be confident that they will have the capacity to provide services in the future. If and when competition and competitive tendering become established the financial viability of a CHE may be undermined. In order to compete to gain a contract CHEs may spend substantially on staff or resources. If that contract is not forthcoming that investment may well not be recoverable. Because of this risk CHEs may be reluctant to develop new services. CHEs also suffer from a lack of capital resources, which gives other providers an advantage in being able to purchase and develop the latest technology to secure contracts. Furthermore non public providers have the advantage of not being required to provide services and can make the best of benefits.

It is feared that the inequality of status in competition may tempt CHEs to increase their income by developing services other than those funded by RHAs or by providing private patient services for which they can charge. There are however a number of constraints on this kind of strategy. Policy guidelines stipulate that RHAs should

---

42 Providers were initially granted immunity until 1 July 1994 because of their inexperience in competitive situations. This move was criticised on the grounds that CHE would be able to gain control of the market at an early stage and consequently stifle competition.

negotiate terms with CHEs to ensure that public funding is not used by others, other than those covered by purchase agreements, and that services would not be delayed or reduced as a result of any other contracts.

CHEs are also required to inform users which publicly funded services are available and the timing and terms of access before any offer of any private treatment can be made. Protocols also provide that CHEs may only provide treatment to private patients if there is surplus capacity. This is dependent on current RHA contracts being fulfilled not on the abolition of waiting lists. Thus, there is a built in requirement for CHEs to have sufficient capacity to allow them to earn extra income and consequently a built in policy to control numbers and waiting times for publicly funded cases. If CHEs choose or find it necessary to increase the level of private income intense negotiation with RHAs would follow. To safeguard public services, however, s 51 looms where there is no negotiated settlement.[43]

The real danger is that CHEs will be tempted to enhance profits by making cuts to the quality of services which RHAs might find difficult to detect. This puts consumers in a difficult position. Service failures that arise from inadequate hospital facilities may give rise to an action under the Consumer Guarantee Act (1993), but this may only be speculation.

Another concern for the certainty and potential viability of CHEs is the practice of at least one RHA to reserve the right in contracts to withdraw from particular services once competition becomes possible.

COMMUNITY TRUSTS

In contrast to the profit making approach of CHEs community trusts may also be established as providers to reflect local requirements and make use of local community facilities. These are non-profit organisations which operate under a trust deed which requires that any surplus be reinvested in health care. Trusts are not government guaranteed and may compete directly with CHEs for contracts with RHAs or may provide services to CHEs on a subcontracting basis.

---

43   Flood and Trebilcock *supra* note 33.

PUBLIC HEALTH

There have been persistent concerns about the provisions for public health in New Zealand and the inequality in access to services. The Health and Disability Services Act initiated a number of changes which have both direct and indirect effects on public health. A main justification for these structural changes in the public health sector was the acknowledgment that some area health boards had sanctioned the use of funds earmarked for public health for treatment services.

Some services, such as immunisation strategy, which previously came under public health organisation, were transferred to RHAs at the outset of the reforms. But, health protection, promotion and disease prevention in general terms were initially provided by a new structure which was hoped would avoid the persistent problem of acute short term health needs detracting from longer term prevention programmes.[44] Funding of public health services, which are primarily promotional and preventative in nature, was separated from personal health care services and the purchaser and provider roles within the former were likewise separated.

The purchasing function for public health services was initially carried out by the Public Health Commission (PHC) which was located within the Department of Health so that the sharing of information could be facilitated, but which was expected to operate with a high degree of independence. The Commission managed the budget for public health activities and developed public health regulations and programmes.

The PHC had central responsibility for public health in the new structure and held the purse strings so that the public health budget would not be high-jacked by other interests. But it is often impossible to separate personal health services from public health initiatives. Many health care providers have to play a key role in meeting public health goals and although regarded as individual health care interventions immunisation and screening programmes, for which RHAs were made responsible are essentially public health matters. The principles of public health consequently have to be adhered to in providing many services and in practice divisions are arbitrary and artificial.

It was also argued that the role of the PHC in monitoring and evaluating the state of public health and setting objectives might be hampered by the requirement that the Commission also purchase

---

44 *Your Health and the Public Health* (Statement of Government Health Policy, July 1991).

services. Furthermore, the PHC had no mandate to demand all the necessary data to evaluate health status and there were no incentives for the sharing of information in the interests of public health. As indicated earlier the PHC was subsumed into the Ministry of Health in December 1994 and the responsibility for the purchase of the majority of public health services passed to RHAs. Bandaranayake has commented that the New Zealand government's record on major public health issues such as tobacco advertising and sponsorship underlines a lack of real concern and does not bode well for the nation's health. He added that the reforms to the public health sector reflected attitudes that denied the basic requirement for including the public as partners in a dialogue for health and health care decision-making as a whole.[45]

CORE HEALTH SERVICES

A significant feature of the New Zealand health care reforms is the provision for the stipulation of core services. Prior to the reforms there was no definition of the services to be provided by public funding. Although a certain amount of prioritising took place this was tacit rather than explicit and as in the UK, services were in effect rationed through fixed budgets and waiting lists. There was also regional variation in the accessibility of services.

The purpose of the core list was to define more explicitly which services RHAs and other health care plans should offer to their consumers. However, core services are not intended necessarily either to be free or immediate, although the New Zealand government indicated that it would ensure that any user charges for core services would be affordable and waiting times would be reasonable and appropriate. The two justifications for establishing a core list of services was first to elicit what has happened to the money spent on health and disability services and second to find out which services New Zealanders thought were the most important. In other words the definition of core services was perceived as assisting the setting of priorities in terms of both value of services to the population and value for money.

The National Advisory Committee on Core Health and Disability Support Services was appointed in March 1992 to represent the views of the community to the government and give independent advice on which services should be purchased in order for people to have access

---

45 D Bandaranayake 'Public Health Without the Public', in *Health Reforms: A Second Opinion* 1992.

on fair terms, with respect to fiscal limits. The Committee has a number of key tasks:

- to seek to identify current services in terms of their costs, their efficiency, the range available, their utilisation, and any deficiencies or variations in their provision;

- to assess the effectiveness and relative benefits of these services and the potential impact of any recommended changes;

- to consult with the public and with health professionals and other relevant persons about the services currently provided and their distribution, and to seek views on which services the government should ensure are purchased, how they should be distributed and the terms of access on which they should be available;

- to recommend periodically to the Minister of Health any changes necessary in the future processes for advising the government on core health and disability support services.[46]

The first report of the Committee in October 1992 set out the current health and disability support services, the broad priorities identified from consultations held with the public during September and October of that year and other representations received through questionnaires, discussion documents and other submissions. Guidelines for RHAs to improve the effectiveness of health outcomes and equity of access in some specific areas of service were also issued. These guidelines were developed by groups of expert professionals and lay people through a consensus conference process.

The Committee's main recommendation was that the current provision of health and disability support services should be the baseline for services purchased by RHAs for 1993/94. They saw little merit in drawing up a detailed list in some kind of priority order. The Committee pointed out that present provision, for the most part, reflected fairly accurately the values and priorities and common sense decision-making of several past generations. This was not to say that current provision was perfect or that modifications should not be made, but rather that changes should be well researched and gradual. They recommended that RHAs should provide purchase plans and report on service differences where any innovative provision would result in shifts from the baseline. This would allow RHAs to contract for better ways of providing services rather than being constrained by current arrangements.

---

46 *Core Health and Disability Support Services for 1993/94* (First Report of the National Advisory Committee on Core Health and Disability Support Services, October 1992).

The Committee was asked to report at a very early stage of their work. They recognised that more consistent and better information needed to be available if quality decisions were to be made about core services in the future. Although the Committee commented that the information and data available were more comprehensive than before it currently raised more questions than it answered. The Committee also stated that it intended to look at what criteria should be applied to determine the benefit derived from services so that they might be admitted or deleted from the core. They also recognised that more public consultation needed to be undertaken in order to obtain a more complete view of New Zealanders' priorities on health and disability support services. They undertook to study further the regional differences identified in the first report and to seek to improve the balance between services. There was a perceived need to re-balance resources between primary and secondary care and between community based and institutional services.

They consequently made recommendations about the information they believed it was essential to collect and stated that the Department of Health, RHAs and the Core Services Committee needed to co-operate in defining and collecting that information.

The Committee's programme in their second year built on that carried out in 1992. They continued to consult widely, in a variety of ways, to develop their advice. They had also considered further the appropriateness of a list approach to core services and rejected it. The Committee argued that such an approach was overly simplistic and potentially unfair because it might ignore the benefit of a particular service to a particular patient at a particular time. They considered that the question of core services is not so much *which* services should be publicly funded but *whether and when* a service should be publicly funded. Specific recommendations were made in relation to managing waiting lists and waiting times, the provision of high technology and specialist care services, primary care practice and the integration of planning for health and disability support services. The recommendations for 1994/5 had five main objectives:

- that the present range of health services and disability support services, as specified in each RHAs funding agreement with the Department of Health should continue, with the emphasis on ensuring the best outcomes for patients and clients by identifying services for pubic funding which provide the most overall benefit;

- to identify and specify those services where regional or national provision is appropriate for reasons of quality or safety and where rationalisation of high technology facilities is required to minimise expensive duplication;

- to identify other services where it is appropriate for there to be a high degree of local determination to meet local population needs in each RHA;

- within the constraints of existing funding to ensure full public funding for services which are available only in overseas facilities (eg liver transplants), so they are available on the same fair terms as fully funded services provided in New Zealand;

- to confirm the six areas identified by the community in 1992 as priorities. The Committee confirmed that RHAs should give increasing emphasis in purchasing decisions to mental health and substance abuse services, children's health, integrated and community care, emergency ambulance, habilitation and rehabilitation and hospice services.[47]

Also in this second report the Committee began to consider services provided by the voluntary sector and complementary medicine. The Committee intends to undertake a further stocktake of services and the effects of purchasing decisions which should progressively better meet the needs of people in each region in 1994/5 and will report their findings in the 1996 report. Besides outlining recommendations from the Committee to the New Zealand government, the second report identified areas for further discussion which had become apparent from consultation processes and also set out the next steps that the committee intended to take in its on-going work to define core services, including the ethical and moral issues associated with identifying priorities.

As the Committee has found, the definition of core services is problematic and raises a number of issues, not least the requirement that any limitation of services be consistent with ethical principles.

Once the reforms to structures, RHAs, CHEs and community trusts and the purchaser/provider separation has become established it was initially proposed to introduce a voucher scheme. Those who might prefer a different approach to health care than that offered by the RHAs would be able to 'opt out' and obtain all their health services through a health care plan of their choice. Such people would be able to utilise their entitlement to government funding for health care to pay an annual fee for a health care plan.[48] RHAs would become, in effect, a state controlled health plan and would be expected to compete in the market for customers alongside private operators.

---

47 *Core Health and Disability Support Services for 1994/95* (Second Report of the National Advisory Committee on Core Health and Disability Support Services, August 1993).

48 *Your Health and the Public Health* (Statement of Government Health Policy, July 1991) p 161.

To overcome concerns often associated with private insurance schemes and to encourage health care plan operators to fund the sick as opposed to the healthy, those with higher health care costs would be able to receive a higher proportion of funding. Besides providing standard comprehensive cover it was argued that health care plans would be able to provide the flexibility necessary to meet the diverse needs of the population by concentrating on certain 'packages' at particular times of life (eg elderly care, or maternity needs). Thus, they would provide for the total health care requirements of their clients and would contract with health care providers to provide this care, although they may provide some services themselves. As in the UK a prime objective of the changes in New Zealand is to give others, particularly general practitioners, a major role in shaping primary, secondary and community health care and to counter the perceived dominance of specialists in service development. A health plan scheme was seen as one of the ways of facilitating this.

Health care plans might be established around groups of general practices, Maori organisations, large firms or other configurations. However, health care plans would not be government guaranteed which could undermine to some extent the governments intentions that no one should be without medical care. However, those who wished to do so would be allowed to return to the government scheme.

The establishment of health care plans was part of the latter part of New Zealand's health system reforms and has not yet been implemented. It seems increasingly unlikely that there will be any change to the number of purchasing organisations in the foreseeable future as the New Zealand government has been heavily criticised by national providers over the high level of bureaucracy already inherent in the health reforms.

CONTRACTS

Contracting out of hospital ancillary services began in New Zealand some 50 years ago, but was largely confined to cleaning and other 'hotel services'.[49] Contracting for more technical services is beset by long-standing difficulties in pricing health services. The necessary information systems are only in the early stages of development in New Zealand. As in the UK patterns of contracting, in the first year, closely followed previous commitments.

---

49   Stubbs and Barnett, 'Privatisation of Public Hospital Ancillary Services' (1992) in *Changing Places in New Zealand: a Geography of Restructuring* (Britton, Le Heron and Pawson Eds).

The New Zealand system uses formal written contracts to mediate the relationship between RHAs and providers. There are a number of significant differences between New Zealand's health care contracts and those of the NHS. Whilst both are likely to reflect the same complexities due to the inherent nature of health care they are not subject to the same legal conundrums. New Zealand's health care contracts are legally binding, giving rise to contractual rights and obligations which can be tested in court. Further, because of the provisions of the Privity Contract Act (1986) third parties are able to sue on contracts in New Zealand.

However, resort to litigation is intended to be a last resort. In the event of a dispute between an RHA and provider, continuity of service is fundamental so that users are not inconvenienced whilst the matter is resolved. Contracts and other arrangements therefore are expected to make specific provision for dispute resolution. In contrast to their counterparts in the UK, RHAs in New Zealand have jointly developed a dispute resolution procedure which is set out in Health Sector Mediation and Arbitration Rules[50] and is for use in all contracts. RHAs are keen to settle disputes where possible by negotiation prior to it being referred to formal mediation or arbitration. Key points are:

- parties will endeavour to settle the dispute or differences between themselves;

- if agreement cannot be reached the dispute will be referred to a mediator or, if necessary an arbitrator;

- if the dispute cannot be settled by agreement or mediation the decision of the arbitrator will be final.[51]

The degree of real competition which may be achieved poses a further potential problem with health sector contracts. The Minister for Health has indicated that contracts should not be awarded on an individual basis, but s 27 of the Commerce Act (1986), to which the health care sector is subject, prohibits arrangements or contracts which substantially lessen competition.

Purchasing of services from providers is undertaken throughout the year as not all contracts are concluded at the beginning of the funding period. RHAs need the flexibility to be responsive to needs and opportunities that might arise during the year. Contracts may however last for longer than a year.

---

50 *Health Sector Mediation and Arbitration Rules* (1993)

51 *Statement of Intent* (Central Regional Health Authority, July 1994) p 27.

There are inherent difficulties in contracting for health services, specifically those pertaining to clinical care. The volume and quality of the end product cannot be easily specified, transaction costs are generally high, there are often large economies of scale and there may be few financial benefits for specialisation. Benefits to be gained from contracting also depend on there being competition amongst providers of services. This is not always feasible to any extent in the health sector and providers are more readily able to call the tune with purchasers. Consequently considerations which give rise to advantages in contracting are not often met with in health markets. The problem is that:

> providing human services of high quality on a sustained basis is so different from the problem of producing standardised products at a fixed price (such as automobiles) that it calls into question the simple proposition that government could increase its general effectiveness by stimulating competition by purchasing services.[52]

Further, there are difficulties in designing a contract that can account for unforeseeable future changes in service objectives or technology, input costs and other factors and building needed flexibility into a contract can give opportunities for abuse of monopoly power. Those who already hold contracts have an advantage over competitors when contracts come up for renewal. Not only may there be a reluctance to cause disruption to service supply by switching contractors,[53] but a current contract holder already has access to relevant assets, has a specialised staff, and is better informed about operating costs. Smith and Lipsky point out that contracting out will not be efficient where it is important that there be a continuing relationship between the provider and the patient, eg long term therapeutic care such as mental heath services. They also note that where a long-term relationship is required the public agency will forge close ties with private providers.[54]

There are also political factors which are likely to come into play. RHAs may be reluctant to withdraw contracts from CHEs even in the face of more efficient competitors because CHEs may not remain viable without gaining several substantial contracts. It would not generally be politically acceptable nor necessarily in the RHA interest to let the CHE become insolvent. From this perspective the government vision of two independent entities periodically contracting in the market on a basis of price and quality alone looks implausible.

---

52   Smith and Lipsky, 'Privatisation in Health and Human Services: a Critique' (1992) *Journal of Health Politics* 17:2 Policy and Law 233.

53   Williamson, *The Economic Institutions of Capitalism* (1985) Chapter 13.

54   Smith and Lipsky *op cit* p 245.

Health sector contracts in New Zealand, as in the UK, are subject to a range of difficulties, which although perhaps not insurmountable present challenges with regard to establishing a viable competitive market. The problem is compounded by the professional and political vested interests of most of the parties involved and a somewhat subjective emotional factor peculiar to the subject of health services. Contracts are now meant to translate local needs into effective services, but these may be costly to monitor and remedial action unsatisfactory and possibly too late.

Government examples of contracts were criticised as being simple and procedure-oriented with predictable costs, volume and outcome probabilities and were consequently unrepresentative of the bulk of health care for which information is not currently available.[55] There is also concern that as contracts in New Zealand are legally binding and enforceable CHEs will decline to enter into those which might impose serious constraints on them. Legally binding contracts also bring the health services within the jurisdiction of commercial law, not only does the already mentioned Commerce Act (1986) apply, but the dominant position of RHAs and CHEs in the market renders the Fair Trading Act applicable. The Consumer Guarantee Act, which relates to the supply of services, may also apply. In professional services there is a guarantee that the service will be of such a nature and quality that it can reasonably be expected to achieve any particular result that the consumer expressly or by implication makes known to the supplier. These Acts could have profound implications for the operation and delivery of New Zealand health care.

QUALITY AND ACCOUNTABILITY

Responsibilities for monitoring the quality of health care provision rests with RHAs. However, the assessment of quality of service in the restructured health environment is currently one of the least defined areas. The New Zealand government established a Steering group composing a representative arm; the Department of Health, the Health Reform Directorate, the NIPB and the National Advisory Committee on Core Health Services, to examine how quality in health services could be ensured in the new system. Terms of reference included the examination of mechanisms for ensuring quality, including those already established such as legislation providing for licensing and the former area health board protocols.

---

55 J Morton, *Tied up with contracts* 1994.

Possible means of assessing quality include audit, peer review and accreditation. An awareness of the value of incorporating quality assurance and quality management systems is in its infancy in New Zealand and many providers appear to be struggling with the concepts of quality assurance, Total Quality Management, accreditation and so forth. In addition, many professional groups are in the process of developing peer review and other quality assurance programmes.[56]

There are five main ways in which quality assurance is determined in the health sector in New Zealand, three of which are mandatory, two voluntary. The first is through performance requirements stipulated in contracts with RHAs and monitored by them. Accordingly, RHAs have developed in-house routine performance monitoring systems and some capacity for audit of providers compliance with purchase agreement quality requirements.

The second is through monitoring of regulatory requirements through the Ministry of Health Licensing Offices. Besides meeting RHA contractual requirements many providers must also obtain a licence from the Ministry. Much of the legislation relating to health and disabilities however dates from the 50s and 60s and has not kept pace with the changes within the health sector. Consequently, the legislation is currently being reviewed and updated. One of the aims of the review is to streamline the regulatory regime and incorporate the changes put in place by the health reforms.

The third method is through requirements placed on CHEs by the Crown Company Monitoring Advisory Unit (CCMAU) The CCMAU have various means of attempting to affirm and measure the quality of care delivered. The main means are a series of performance indicators on which hospitals must report. The measures were developed with significant input from CHE management, clinicians, CCMAU business analysts and the CCMAU Clinical Advisory Group which comprises a group of eminent senior clinicians and management. The development of measures is an on-going process due to improvements in information systems, changing consensus about definitions and the changing need of CHEs.[57]

The two voluntary ways are by accreditation or by developing a quality management system unique to the organisation. Accreditation is a comprehensive system of measuring every aspect of hospital performance. The two largest accreditation systems available in New Zealand are; the New Zealand Council on Health Care Standards,

---

56   Sylvia Sax, Senior Analyst, Quality Southern Regional Health Authority.
57   CHE: Framework for Performance Measurement System (*CCMAU*, February 1995).

which was established in 1990 and which has drafted standards and developed education programmes on quality specifically for New Zealand and the ISO-900 series. Accreditation operates primarily as an external audit, and standards are rewritten annually. Awarding of accreditation requires commitment and expense on the part of the hospital and is valid for three years, after which time hospitals must reapply. Whilst all four RHAs emphasise the importance of providers demonstrating a commitment to delivering and improving quality services they also consider that accreditation remain voluntary. The reason for this is that were accreditation to become mandatory all providers would be required to comply with these standards. If purchasing a service were dependent on the provider attaining accreditation there would be pressure to accredit providers even if standards were not adequately met.[58] Accreditors are reluctant to withhold accreditation from providers because it would mean that those organisations would lose a large proportion of business. This is particularly so in a competitive environment. Sax points out that research and experience in other countries has indicated that the best results occur when accreditation is taken up out of a commitment to quality within the organisation rather than when it becomes an end in itself.

Finally, a word on peer review which has traditionally played a major role in determining quality of both clinical and research medical services and remains a very strong mechanism for maintaining certain standards. The public perception of peer review and confidence in this process in New Zealand was undermined when the Cartwright Report was published in 1988.[59] There may consequently be problems regarding the efficacy of peer review as a means of quality control in a competitive health market. However, confidence in the procedure may be bolstered by the appointment of the Health and Disabilities Commissioner who has the power to investigate complaints on behalf of the individual.

APPOINTMENTS TO HEALTH BODIES

It has been suggested that the reality behind the rhetoric of consumer choice, markets and devolution is that whilst providers, as contractors, may win more freedom in certain areas, executive power also

---

58   S Sax 'Accreditation – a purchasers perspective' (March 1995) *Health Manager* Vol 2 No 1.
59   The Report of the Cervical Cancer Inquiry.

increases.[60] At the same time the power of intermediate institutions, such as the medical profession is diminished and more closely regulated. Appointments made to Boards responsible for effecting the restructuring generally reflected, at least in terms of leadership, persons who were strongly committed to the proposals of the New Zealand government. As in the UK those appointed to Boards have considerable business experience and of particular interest was the composition of the CHEs. Key criteria for selection were stated to be sound commercial knowledge and an understanding of the local economic and social structures of each area. The membership of all committees reflects large numbers of management consultants, accountants, and a sprinkling of lawyers. Commercial enterprise, at least in some aspects, is to be welcomed, but at the same time the appointment of only one health professional appears surprising, given that appointments have also included five farmers. The only committee to reflect a balanced membership with a range of expertise is the National Advisory Committee on Core Health Services and Disability Support Services. It appears that devolution may not be as real as is suggested, given that the government remains ultimately responsible for the funding of health services. Whether increased local autonomy is in fact a spurious autonomy has yet to be determined.

THE PLACE OF THE HEALTH CARE CONSUMER

Promotion and protection of the rights to health and disability care has been strengthened by the enactment of the Health and Disability Commissioner Act (1994). The Act has four main parts which allow the setting up or appointment of:

- an independent Commissioner to carry out the purpose of the Act. New Zealand's first Health and Disability Commissioner was appointed in December 1994. The initial step to be undertaken by the Commissioner is to develop through consultation;

- a Code of Rights which will apply to all types of health and disability services whether paid for or not. Once the final draft Code has been prepared it will be submitted to the Minister of Health who is responsible for enacting it;[61]

---

60 D Hughes *The Reorganisation of the National Health Service: the Rhetoric and the Reality of the Internal Market* (1991) 54 MLR.

61 At the time of writing, the Commissioners aim is to present the draft Code to the Minister by the end of October 1995.

- locally based advocacy services to assist users in resolving complaints;

- a complaints process which enables the independent investigation, mediation and prosecution of *breaches of the Code*.

The Code of Rights, which is the crux of the legislation, is to be drawn up by the Health and Disability Commissioner in consultation with community and provider groups. There are a number of issues under consideration against which health organisations may be measured including informed choice and consent, information on services, privacy and complaints handling, cultural safety and continuity of care which are presently incorporated into an informal statement of intent and which are likely to form part of the framework of the Code.

However the public has no legal right to particular services within their region, nor are levels of service guaranteed. The focus of the Act is on procedural rights and the process of delivery, concerned with the way patients have been treated rather than any entitlement to services. The Act is not a means therefore for enhancement of collective choice or protest about the particular services or mix of services purchased.[62]

Informed choice and consent

People should be given a clear explanation of their condition and any treatment proposed, including any risks and any alternative treatments, before they decide whether they will agree to that treatment. People should also choose whether or not they wish to take part in medical research or medical student training.

These issues are incorporated into the New Zealand Bill of Rights Act (1990) which affirms that everyone has the right to refuse to undergo any medical treatment and not be subject to medical experimentation. Informed choice and consent is a process aimed at ensuring that this occurs. The New Zealand government has recognised that effective communication and provision of appropriate information are integral to the enhancement of autonomy and that because of inequality in the relationship between providers and users it is the health professional who has the primary responsibility for providing information to make informed choices.[63]

Not only do the public need information to be able to make a rational decision about their own treatment but accountability requires that information be given, for example, on quality standards and

---

62 D Stephenson 'The Contracting Process – Building New Relationships in Health Care' Commentary in *Contracting in the Health Sector* see *supra* (note 2).

63 *Purchasing for Your Health* (Ministry of Health, 1993–4).

maximum waiting times to enable judgments to be made about the performance of health providers and local services. To that end purchase plans and locality plans are to be published and the Performance Monitoring and Review Unit of the Department of Health is to publish an annual report.

But the provision of information can be valueless if there are no channels by which to put that information to use in policy decisions. The development of real consultative and participative processes is essential if the potential value of information is to be encashed.

Development of participation is of course closely allied to respect for the diversity and expression of people's beliefs. In New Zealand respect for cultural and religious beliefs is expressed in the concept of 'cultural safety' and is embodied in the Treaty of Waitangi, the country's founding document. The concept of cultural safety is the protection from physical, psychological, social and spiritual harm that can occur when cultural factors are ignored or unsatisfactorily accounted for in the identification, purchase and delivery of public services. In a policy statement of 1992 the government outlined what it expected of health purchasers in respect of cultural safety for Maori, and has produced two specific Maori Policy Guideline documents.[64]

Complaints

During 1993/4 the government required CHEs, if they had not already done so, to establish customer complaints services. RHAs through their purchase agreements also require CHEs and other major providers to maintain a complaints system which are audited by RHAs.[65] Regions have established their own systems to support those operated by providers to allow people a choice in how their complaints are heard. This includes having staff specifically dedicated to working through the issues with members of the community. Northern Region have set up a free phone 'hot line' which patients may use to lodge complaints or seek information and Midland Region has contracted with the Health Consumer Service to provide a complaints mediation service.[66] RHAs are also using independent agencies, such as patient advocacy services to monitor consumer complaints.

---

64 *Whaia te ora mo te iwi: Strive for the good health of the people* (1992) and *Policy Guidelines for Maori Health* (1994/5 and 1995/96).

65 Southern Region conducted a detailed audit of the complaints processes of major providers in their area to ensure good internal procedures and highlight effective of informing usershow to make a complaint.

66 In 1993/4 this service resolved 470 complaints by personnel intervention and a similar number by phone or correspondence.

CONCLUSION

The purposes of the New Zealand reforms as set out in s 4 of the Health and Disability Services Act are to be applauded. But these purposes could well be undermined by the qualification that they are to be attained in the context of what is reasonably achievable within the amount of funding provided. Financial concerns are of course always a paramount consideration. It is not possible for all the services that people would like to be provided. It is arguable that by framing objectives explicitly within a financial context New Zealand is more honest than most. However this does not detract from the basic democratic principle to consult and enable the public to have an input into policy choices and the setting of appropriate standards of care. In other words public input is crucial to the legitimacy of decisions about what is reasonably achievable.

Effective consultation can lift policy choices from vested interests and can ensure real input into the purchasing decisions of RHAs as well as their funding agreements with government. In this way RHAs would overcome the lack of independence from the Ministry of Health and the tendency of contracting to submerge policy decisions relevant to purchasing would be diminished.[67]

The present re-organisation of health care in New Zealand has some worthwhile features but it is arguable that these could have been incorporated into the area health boards system. As with any change in public policy there are winners and losers when effects on the public and the choices available to them are taken into account. With RHAs free to purchase services from any provider, consumers may find themselves able to use a wider range of facilities than the public hospitals run previously by the area health boards. However for those with community service cards,[68] the choice of general practitioner could be gradually diminished if all general practitioners are not contracted to provide services and they can no longer provide subsidised services.

As with the NHS, the main issue is not the introduction of contracting nor the provision of the purchaser/provider split, but the pro-competitive stance of the New Zealand reforms and the lack of understanding that contracting can have a value of its own, free from

---

67 Freedland *Government by Contract and Public Law* [1994] PL Spring pp 86, 98-99.

68 Matheson in 'Falling Short of Target', *Health Reforms; a Second Opinion* (see *supra* note 9), points out that there are an increasing number of people encountering difficulty in gaining access to health care due to constraints on receiving a card.

competition, in the promotion of the public interest through open negotiation for good quality and effective health services.

In addition, worthy of note is the attempt to integrate primary, secondary and community care. A well co-ordinated health care system depends on good co-operative relationships between all providers. But whilst the reforms integrate funding of health services, the competitive model means that the integration of delivery may not occur. The Core Health Services and Disability Committee also has merit and has resisted trying to identify what it considers is not possible. It is to be hoped that it does not meet the same fate as the Public Health Commission.

However, the roles of the various agencies concerned in the purchasing and the provision of health services needs to be clarified and health objectives should be stated explicitly. Of fundamental importance are the establishment of mechanisms for public input. Bandaranayake argues that the individual concept of self-advancement evident in current changes goes against the basic and established tenets of public health practice.[69] The essence of his criticism is that for the improvement and maintenance of health status:

the people have the right and duty to participate individually and collectively in the planning and implementation of their health care.[70]

Ironically, the original Green and White Paper identified a lack of consumer control and the feeling that there was too little consultation, as one of the main problems of the previous system.[71]

Effective community consultation and input requires a population that is informed. Yet there is a real risk that information is harder to get as competition intensifies. A former New Zealand ombudsman noted that after corporatisation of other state bodies there was an erosion of the right to access to information of public interest. She saw that it was difficult to obtain from commercially minded organisations information that had previously been in the public sector. The new system provides for the collection and processing of information about consumers which should be of assistance to purchasers and providers in planning but will not always be available publicly.

The reforms have a reduced role for health promotion and consequently fail to take account of policies on employment, housing, education, welfare benefits and their potential adverse impact on

---

69 D Bandaranayake *Public Health Without the Public (ibid)*.

70 WHO Primary Health Care; report of the international conference on primary health care: USSR 1978

71 *Your Health and the Public Health* (Statement of government policy, 1991).

health, discarding non economic values such as equity, acceptability and appropriateness of services.

> the preoccupation with issues of quality and access, the continued adherence to the disease-oriented model of health care, a complete lack of emphasis on identifying and meeting population health needs, the artificial separation of preventive and treatment services, a lack of integration with primary care services and the distance of policy makers and purchasers from the coal face, all add up to a recipe for disaster on the public health front.[72]

Ironically, area health boards were beginning to develop policies which embraced the broader social and educational factors of health. In short it can be argued that the New Zealand reforms have replaced democratic institutions with ministerial appointed boards, uncertain provisions for consultation and a complex network of contracts that could confuse rather than clarify the location of responsibility for health services.

---

72   *ibid.*

CHAPTER 4

THE NATIONAL HEALTH SERVICE

INTRODUCTION

The National Health Service (NHS) like other public organisations has tended to look increasingly to technical and managerial solutions to solve its difficulties. Because of the constitutional background of the UK the legal system and public law in particular has made little contribution to the development of any means which might enhance what could be termed administrative or organisational 'due process' in public services. Fuelled and misled by the myth of public accountability, that government is answerable to citizens through Parliament, there has been a failure to come to terms with the need to develop surrogate political processes to facilitate a rational foundation for collective and individual choice in modern policy making. Consequently there has been little consideration of the possibility of looking to *constitutional* principles to help solve the problems of management of public services, leaving the way open for incremental and reactive conduct which has often been based on an inadequate analysis and superficial debate of options. This is no less true of the health service.[1]

When the National Health Service (NHS) was founded in 1948 a miscellaneous host of private, municipal and charitable health providers were merged into an institution which has become highly specialised. Description of its formal structure understates the complexity and opacity of decision-making processes within the organisation and the way in which choices are made about the selection of priorities and the utilisation of resources. From the beginning, public accountability has been a shadowy concept and there have been recurring difficulties in reconciling public input with the other, often diverse interests which manifest themselves in the structure of the NHS.

The declared aims of the NHS at its formation were exemplary; they were to promote better health, to ensure equal access to care and to provide comprehensive coverage, free at the point of entry. Market allocation of resources was specifically rejected at that time as health care was considered to be a matter of social entitlement to be both funded and provided publicly. By providing an organisational

---

1   D Longley, *Public Law and Health Service Accountability* (Open University Press, 1993).

framework for the *national* co-ordination of the allocation and distribution of resources the NHS was considered to be an expedient and relatively economic solution to the enormous health care task. Despite contentious debates prior to the enactment of the National Health Service Act (1946) and initial dissension from the medical profession about a number of aspects of the new health care scheme, the initial aims of the NHS continue to command substantial support and respect from all quarters.

In many ways the NHS has proved a successful enterprise. It has displayed many major strengths; comparatively, it is comprehensive, equitable and accessible and by international standards has provided relatively good quality care for low overhead costs. But as in Canada and New Zealand the sheer scale and diversity of the health services that are needed, the continual development of highly technical procedures for diagnosis and treatment, not to mention the toll of ever increasing demand and expectations, have exerted recurrent pressures which have led to severe problems in sustaining and at times even attaining the worthy primary objectives of the NHS.

In addition to the difficulties arising from medical inflation, almost from the outset there was a continual problem in the NHS with overall planning, co-ordination and balance between the different parts of the service. As elsewhere, resource utilisation became dominated by the medical profession in the acute sector, which grew rapidly at the expense of the primary. The tradition of clinical autonomy combined with continual financial pressures also made planning a difficult task. There were also few mechanisms either to determine the actual costs of services or gauge the appropriateness of medical activity. As a result, the NHS has been the subject of a number of reports which have highlighted 'a continuing degree of uncertainty about the necessary organisational, administrative and financial consequences of the ideals and aspirations of the service'.[2] But these have never really come to grips with whether or not there is some intrinsic instability underpinning the NHS and have been content to leave its formal administrative configuration for the most part untouched.

Throughout the 1970s and 80s a whole series of well documented, pragmatic and incremental changes were put in place at various times in response to these difficulties. These typically focused on the need to strengthen the NHS management structure and placed an increasing emphasis on the containment of costs, but there was really little consideration given to the overall implications of these moves. Initial changes were concerned with achieving savings primarily in the non-

---

2   Carrier and Kendall, *Socialism and the NHS, Avebury* (Gower Publishing, 1990) p 4.

clinical areas of health services, only in more recent years were attempts made to involve clinicians in taking a share of responsibility for operating within budgetary limits. However, clinical activity proved difficult to call to account. Not only were information schemes inadequate and unreliable but there were no real means of applying the degree of pressure sufficient to alter the work patterns and practices of doctors.

Health policy continued to be characterised quite substantially by uncertainty and contradiction and there was a failure to develop any significant objectives for gains in health overall. From inside and outside the health services the purpose and the effectiveness of some of the 'efficiency improving' measures that had been imposed were questioned and the criticism that in reality savings were only being achieved through cuts in services rather than through any sustained improvements in efficiency, was increasingly expressed.

As regards public and individual choice, as health care spending failed to be contained within the cash limits prescribed by government, health care provision itself was constrained by means which were less than explicit. Service rationing and hence health policy, came to be more a result of tacit action than any open and reasoned choice. As waiting lists grew so did the dissatisfaction of both health service professionals and the public.

Matters eventually reached a critical point in the late 1980s when financial constraints led to quite overt cut-backs in hospital services and a number of well publicised judicial review cases.[3] Around that time several influential reports were also published which lent support to the view that there had been a legacy of under investment in health care. The resulting widespread and quite vociferous unease prompted the review of the NHS which subsequently formed the basis of the most fundamental reform of the system to have taken place since its inception. This review was not however the exercise in public consultation which marked the preparation of the Canadian health reforms. The UK government refused to set up a Royal Commission and proceeded to carry out an investigation of the NHS in secret, headed by the Prime Minister, Margaret Thatcher. The names of other members of the review team were not made public until after the publication of the White Paper Working for Patients[4] which outlined government intentions.

The underlying aim of the reforms of the 90s is stated to be the decentralisation of power and a concomitant increase in local level

---

3   See D Longley *op cit.*

4   Cmnd 555.

autonomy for the provision and operation of health services. In practice there has been a continuation of a shift to general management and a further strengthening of means to control expenditure. More radically, as is now the case in New Zealand, there has been an introduction of an internal market which has separated the function of purchasing health care from its provision. Whilst both main strands are concerned with increased efficiency and cost effectiveness, the latter is also premised on consumer sovereignty and improvement in quality through competition. The current re-organisation is thus intended to provide a more accountable and efficient service; one which is responsive to community needs, enhances patient choice and results in overall health benefits. Once again the concept is exemplary, the fundamental question, of course, is whether the NHS is now set to deliver health care in a manner which fulfils these expectations.

THE STRUCTURE

From the beginning, the statutory and administrative framework of the NHS, was intended to facilitate the considerable complexities of translating broad objectives into operation at a local level and of turning resources into services. The pattern followed was one familiar to constitutional and public lawyers in that substantive aims and powers are stated only in very general terms and their implementation is left to the relatively unstructured discretion of the health service hierarchy; the Secretary of State, the Department of Health in its several manifestations and the health authorities. The two major re-organisations prior to the present one did little to alter this structure, nor at first sight did the latest reforms appear to depart radically from the traditional format. However some of the changes, particularly those that have come about at the lower end of the NHS structure, have had unprecedented implications for organisational coalitions and the balance of power within the system.

The provision of health care is legally the function of the Secretary of State for Health. Together with the National Health Service Act (1977), which has remained the principal Act, the National Health Service and Community Care Act (1990) (to be referred to as the 1990 Act) has provided the Minister with extremely broad and extensive discretionary powers. However, in common with other areas of public policy the range and complexities of issues involved in running a public organisation, not to mention the difficulties presented by the peripatetic nature of most Ministers' jobs, necessitate the majority of the Secretary of State's powers and duties being exercised by and through the administrative structure of the NHS. Prior to the 1990 Act this structure was clearly hierarchical. All hospital and other health care services were managed directly by district health authorities (DHAs). Above the DHAs in the management structure, until their number was reduced to eight in 1994, there were 14 regional health authorities (RHAs) which, like DHAs, were statutory corporations acting on behalf of the Secretary of State.

The paramount power of the Secretary of State is, of course, the control of NHS expenditure through the use of cash limits. The total amount of funding available to the NHS each year is determined by the Public Expenditure Survey (PES) process and depends on the relative priority given to it by government and the demands of other departments. Until recently, this amount was sub-divided and allocated to health authorities on the basis of a formula which sought to identify the health care needs of each regional population. However, RHAs tended to vary in the extent to which they then relied on this formula to allocate funds to their respective districts and eventually funds were more likely to be distributed on the basis of planned service developments.[5]

The formula was devised at a time when there was expected to be a continuing increase in funding and was intended to make the distribution of resources more equitable. But it came to be applied in a period of financial constraint which meant, paradoxically, that gains could only be made for some districts at the expense of losses for others.[6] The overall result was that there was often no direct correlation between the amount of money a district was allocated and the number of patients it actually had to treat.

Since the 1990–91 financial year, use of the original formula has been discontinued and a modified system of funding has been phased in. Health authorities are now funded on a capitation basis, weighted to reflect the health and age distribution of the population and the relative cost of providing services. The new formulation is not however entirely free of difficulties. A great deal of information about the composition of resident populations, their age and mortality rates, has to be ascertained for the new system to be fully operational and adequate information is not always readily available. Although one of the benefits of a population based allocation scheme is that areas with fast growing populations can be automatically compensated on an annual basis, there is a potential disadvantage that districts with declining populations may progressively receive less money. Some of these latter districts serve areas of social deprivation whose health care

5   *Working for Patients* para 4.5.
6   R Klein *The Politics of the NHS* (Harlow Longman, 1989, 2nd edn) 234.

needs are generally high. If these factors are not effectively monitored and incorporated into calculations so that funding is adjusted, a less than equitable distribution of resources can follow.

Despite the recent introduction of the market culture into the NHS, overall financial control of spending by health services and the distribution of funds remains strictly controlled by the utilisation of cash limits which have statutory force. The regulatory package in fact makes it quite clear that ultimate control lies at the centre where both financial and legal sanctions are available for non-compliance, although these have as yet rarely been put into use.

Much more in issue from the perspective of the concerns expressed in this book are the structures for the legitimacy of policy choices and accountability for delegated decision-making throughout the organisation of the NHS. Formally the Minister carries ultimate responsibility for the exercise of all health service powers through the traditional parliamentary processes of Question Time, the Public Accounts Committee and the Select Committees on Health and on Social Services. Although these committees and the Audit Commission, to which health authorities and NHS trusts are now subject, carry out in-depth investigations and have produced some excellent reports in recent years, both on expenditure and the provision of services, their impact is too often limited by the institutional framework within which they operate. There are no constitutional mechanisms for ensuring that their deliberations are either taken into account or acted upon. As a result, they generally tend to be effective only to the extent that their conclusions are consistent with government policy and their influence and success as guarantors of public accountability is relatively marginal.[7]

Until 1989 the Department of Health was assisted by a Health Supervisory Board and the National Health Service Management Board. Neither of these had any statutory basis, but were established on the recommendation of the Griffiths Inquiry into NHS Management[8] in an attempt to improve central management and provide a rational framework for accountability between the Secretary of State and the Department of the Health on the one hand and health authorities on the other. The Supervisory Board was set up to be a strategic body which was to determine priorities, objectives and policy. The role of the Management Board was intended to be one of overall management, ensuring policy implementation. In practice, as perhaps might be expected from the inherent difficulties of attempting to

---

7   I Harden and N Lewis, *The Noble lie: the British Constitution and the Rule of Law* (1986) pp 106–111.

8   (1983) HMSO.

separate policy and implementation, the delineation of the respective roles and responsibilities of these two bodies was far from clear.

Health authorities had assumed that the establishment of the Management Board indicated the introduction of some degree of autonomy from government control. But civil servants appeared to regard the Board as a means by which to strengthen executive direction of health service management.[9] The overall effect of these developments was a blurring of the lines of accountability and management such that the centre became too involved with detailed operational matters and relatively too little concerned with monitoring policy implementation and its effectiveness. As a result, the Supervisory Board failed to develop as the central strategic force and eventually became defunct, whilst the functions of the Management Board became correspondingly more multi-faceted.

In an attempt to overcome these deficiencies NHS objectives, strategy and finance are now determined, in the light of government policy, with the advice and support of a Policy Board. Central responsibility for operation and management of the health service falls to the NHS Executive (NHSE), a branch of the Department of Health whose remit is to work within the framework set by the Department of Health and the Policy Board.

The Policy Board is chaired by the Secretary of State for Health and operates with a rolling programme. It is intended that the Board should be concerned with the overall pattern and balance of policy and assessment of their effectiveness rather than any detailed formulation of specific policies. The Policy Board draws on the advice and support of the divisions of the Department of Health, namely the Health and Social Services Divisions which have responsibility for the development of policies applied in and throughout the NHS. The terms of reference of the Policy Board are to lend support to ministers and to advise on the determination of strategy within which the NHS Executive (NHSE) will operate. The Board is also expected to issue annual guidelines and set NHSE objectives within available resources, monitor performance and comment on the desirability and feasibility of specific goals proposed for the NHSE.

Initially the government stated that in order to bring a wide perspective to the formulation of policy objectives for the NHS, members would be drawn from industry and commerce as well as government and the health service. Despite there being an overall emphasis on the business and management experience of appointees,

---

9   K Stowe, *On caring for the National Health* (London: Nuffield Provincial Hospital Trust, 1988).

the membership of the Board was a mix of personnel and cultures that might have been expected to produce some interesting bargaining complexities. However, appointment of members was not made openly and their policy deliberations have rarely reached the public arena. Neither policy reports nor the responses of central management have been made the subject of any widespread scrutiny and comment. It is therefore difficult to estimate to what extent the Policy board actually influences policy as opposed to legitimising what the Secretary of State for Health and the Department already has in mind.

In order to be more effective and accountable for high level policy the Board's debates need to be more transparent and procedures need to be put in place to facilitate input from a wider spectrum of interests. But the possibility of this contention ever becoming practice looks increasingly unlikely. In November 1995 it was announced that changes had been made to the composition of the Policy Board in that the four non-executive members drawn from outside the Department of Health had 'stepped down'. The Policy Board now provides a forum in which Ministers and senior managers meet Regional Chairmen to consider current NHS *management* issues. According to the Secretary of State for Health 'Ministers will continue to seek advice from a wide variety of external sources'.[10] But in no sense can the Policy Board be described as having an open, multi-faceted policy advisory capacity, similar to that found in the Canadian provincial health councils. The actual workings of the Policy Board and its relationship with the policy divisions of the Department of Health are likely to remain somewhat of a mystery as the Board becomes increasingly subsumed into central management and possibly meets the same fate as its predecessor, the Health Supervisory Board.

The functions of the NHSE are to issue strategic and operational guidelines to health authorities, to develop and advise the Policy Board of resource policies and needs; propose the distribution of funds to the regions; and deal with pay and personnel issues. It also sets health authority targets and monitors their achievement through regional planning and review processes. The role of the NHSE now includes responsibility for primary care as well as acute and community health services.

Following an internal report which was critical of the structure of the management Executive, the organisation of the NHSE was streamlined in accordance with its core functions.[11] The report argued that although the Executive was well designed to provide advice and

---

10   Department of Health 95/512.

11   Moore, 'Clean Sweep needed to put House in Order' (March 1991) HSJ p 14.

support to ministers and to monitor the provision of health services, it was not particularly well designed to actually manage it. This of course reflects the differences in orientation between civil service and management perspectives of NHS organisation and also mirrors the debates which have underpinned the development of 'Next Steps' agencies in other areas of government business.

The previous eight directorates within the NHSE were reduced to seven and only two directorates, research and development and personnel, remained principally the same as before. A health care directorate has brought together primary, secondary and community care, and a corporate affairs directorate now defines the strategic framework of the NHS. A performance management directorate is responsible for reviewing NHS performance which is meant to reflect objectives which are approved and monitored by the Policy Board on a twice yearly basis.

Within the NHSE a great deal of reliance is placed on the personal accountability of the Chief Executive and the Directors. Besides being directly accountable to the Secretary of State the Chief Executive is the accounting officer for hospital, community and family health services and is expected to attend the Public Accounts Committee and other select committees as and when required. The management Executive must submit to the Secretary of State and the Policy Board an annual plan which is rolled forward each year in addition to an annual report, which includes detail of health authority out-turn. As well as an extension of exchanges of personnel between civil servants in the Department and management of the NHS there have been some considerable changes in culture in the NHSE. On the whole these have been considered to have worked out well, but whether this will continue to be the case following recent reviews of corporate governance remains to be seen.

Much of the burden of implementing the 1990 reforms in their initial phase fell on RHAs. Although from the outset some regional functions were devolved to district authorities, RHAs were directed to concentrate their efforts on allocating financial resources, setting standards, and monitoring and evaluating the effectiveness of health services in their region. This included a string of additional functions which came about as a result of changes to Family Health Services Authority (FHSA) accountability. The meetings between the then Regional General Managers and the NHSE were at the time regarded as the 'power house' of strategic thinking and decisions taken at the annual conference of regional management were fed through this meeting cycle. Regional Chairmen no longer had any management function but were regarded as 'the eyes and ears' of the Minister with whom there was a meeting every other month. Communication between the Department of Health and the NHS was also maintained through joint working parties and meetings with advisory groups and representative national bodies such as the National Association of Health Authorities and Trusts (NAHAT).[12]

Difficulties similar to those experienced in central management in relation to policy processes were also evident within health authorities. In theory health authority members of both regional and district tiers had responsibility for formulating policies and taking strategic decisions and the function of managers and staff was to advise and implement policy and oversee the day to day operation of services. In practice this differentiation was fudged and some overlap and interchangeability existed between the respective roles of the two groups. Gradually, health authorities came to be seen by government as neither truly representative bodies nor proper management bodies.

The government response to these perceived incompatibilities was to place increased reliance on business management skills and decrease the community representation element. Changes were consequently made to the membership of health authorities, ostensibly on the grounds of an intention 'to extend responsibility for complex managerial and contractual issues to a local level'.[13]

Both regional and district tiers were reduced to five non-executive members and up to five executive members, plus a non-executive chair. Chairs of both levels of health authorities and non-executive members of RHAs were appointed by the Secretary of State and DHA non-executive members by the relevant RHA. However, non-executive appointments were made solely on the basis of the skills and experience members could bring to the work of the health authority, rather than for representation of any particular interest group. This has led to an over-emphasis of members from the business community rather than the wider public.[14]

The reduction of wider community representation and the loss by local government authorities of their previous right to appoint members to DHAs has been a cause for concern. If local health authorities are to fulfil their role in identifying local needs and responding to the wishes of the resident population and planning services accordingly improved avenues for consultation and adequate means of local representation need to be present. The arguments for retaining some local authority representation are forceful, as the job of

---

12 C Ham, *The New NHS* (Oxford NAHAT).

13 *Working for Patients* paras 8.3-8.5

14 A survey conducted by the British Medical Association in 1991 found that out of more than 410 non-executive members 164 were from a business background and just 51 from the medical profession.

the local authority representative can be significant in easing collaboration for the planning and financing of community services between health authorities, local authorities and the independent sector. Since the onset of the reforms in 1990 DHAs have been building up alliances with other community agencies concerned with health care to fulfil their new functions as purchasing agents acquiring services on behalf of residents. But these are discretionary and for the most part have been developed on an informal basis, with no regulatory framework to encourage systematic wider public input.

NHS TRUSTS

The culmination of the devolution of management responsibility and decision-making to a local level was the provision in the 1990 Act for the establishment of NHS Trusts as separate legal entities within the NHS, but outside the health authority management structure. Any NHS unit which is actively involved in patient care may apply for Trust status. The definition of an NHS Trust is therefore flexible and may include hospitals, community based services either alone or together with hospitals, ambulance services and even the provision side of DHAs. The management independence of NHS Trusts is intended to enable them to provide health services which respond more effectively to patient needs and improve the quality of service.

> Whilst remaining fully within the NHS, Trusts ... are operationally independent. Trusts have the power to make their own decisions -- right or wrong! – without being subject to bureaucratic procedures, processes or pressure from higher tiers of management.[15]

The establishment of NHS Trusts was seen by government as a means of 'securing a commitment to the local community and encouraging local pride'. Whilst applying for Trust status has been theoretically voluntary it has been actively, if not fiercely, encouraged. Through five years of quite turbulent change in the NHS the creation of Trusts is now almost complete, only 2% of hospitals remaining under district health management.

The term NHS Trust is a term of art which was substituted for the earlier one of self-governing hospital. Trust was seen to have symbolic advantages over its predecessor, in that to some extent it undermines the early assertions that such institutions were 'opting out' of the NHS and at the same time manages to convey the impression they operate

---

15 *Working for Patients* (NHS Trusts: a working guide 2).

for the benefit of the public and not for any profit motive.[16] But NHS Trusts are certainly not trusts in the usual legal sense as they fail to fulfil the necessary legal requirements for that status and are subject to a degree of executive control that no ordinary trust experiences.

Trusts have extensive powers to acquire, own and dispose of assets; borrow subject to an a annual limit; build up reserves; set their own management structures; employ and direct their own staff and determine pay and conditions of service. They are expected to 'compete' for business and earn their revenue from the services they provide. The main source of income comes from contracts with health authorities for the provision of care to residents. Other contracts and revenue come from general practitioner (GP) groups who hold their own budgets and other health authorities, as well as the private health care sector.

Trusts are statutory corporations, run by their own board of directors, who have responsibility for determining overall policy, monitoring implementation and maintaining the financial viability of the Trust. The board consists of a non-executive chairman appointed by the Secretary of State, up to five non-executive directors, two of whom are to be drawn from the local community. 'Local directors' are appointed by the Regional executive, the remainder by the Secretary of State. Where a Trust has a significant commitment to undergraduate medical teaching one non-executive director must be drawn from the relevant University. Chairmen and non-executive members are appointed for periods of up to four years and in contrast to non-executive members of health authorities receive remuneration. Some groups who may have some knowledge of health service activities are not eligible for appointment as non-executive directors including general practitioners (GPs) and their employees, members and employees of health authorities and other health service bodies and employees of trade unions with members who work in the NHS. This provision seems surprising, but is presumably an attempt to deter potential clashes of interest.

There must also be on the board an equal number of executive directors including the chief executive, the director of finance and for the majority of Trusts a medical and a nursing director. Directors are not personally liable for the actions of the board, otherwise their legal status is uncertain.[17] Apart from these requirements at board level,

---

16 D Hughes, 'The Reorganisation of the NHS: the rhetoric and the reality of the internal market' (1991) MLR 54.

17 See J Jacob 'Lawyers go to Hospital' [1991] PL 225.

Trusts are free to develop management arrangements tailored to their own needs.

Trusts are accountable to the Health Secretary via the NHSE and are subject to legislation that applies directly to NHS facilities such as the Hospital Complaints Procedure Act (1985), the Data Protection Act (1984) and the Access to Health Records Act (1990). In addition trusts are expected to take account, amongst others, of relevant EC Directives; the requirements of statutory bodies, advice relating to patient, public or staff safety, personal privacy and patient confidentiality. However, except in relation to grievance handling and arrangements for communicable diseases, instructions and guidance issued by the NHSE does not automatically apply to NHS Trusts. Unless otherwise directed by the Secretary of State, trusts have a discretion whether to follow such guidance. Like health authorities, trusts are not Crown bodies and do not benefit from Crown immunity.

There are three main accountability measures which apply to trusts although their effectiveness as far as overall public accountability is concerned is questionable since, as might be expected, requirements concentrate mainly on fiscal matters. Trusts are required to produce an annual business plan, in which it is expected that plans to develop services, financial projections and capital building plans will be set out. This is not a public document although a summary has to be publicly provided. However the annual report of the previous years performance and accounts is available for public perusal. These annual reports differ greatly in style, structure and size as well as in the comprehensibility and usefulness of the information, financial and otherwise, that they impart. Whilst the scope of the readership, particularly the general public must be taken into account and the fact that not all matters will be of equal concern or appropriate to every Trust, the principle of openness inherent in being able to exercise choice and which is also supposed to underlie the new NHS Codes of Conduct and Accountability, must surely require the reporting of achievements regarding a trust's performance in terms of all its objectives and not merely its financial targets. In short, in its annual report a trust needs to demonstrate how and if it is striking a fair balance between quality of services and expenditure.

Trusts are also required to provide in-year financial monitoring information, a 'small core of statistical data necessary to support Ministers public accountability for the NHS as a whole', information on capital schemes requiring management Executive or Treasury approval and annual reports under the AIDS (Control) Act (1987). They must also inform the NHSE if their long term financial viability is at risk.

NHS BOARDS

The restructuring of health service boards generated substantial criticism. The view that the process of appointment to board membership was subject to personal and political patronage was widespread. This ran alongside general and growing concern about standards of conduct in the public sector and appointments to quangos. Following serious managerial failures in at least two health authorities which had been highlighted by the National Audit Office[18] amongst others, the NHS Chief Executive set up a task force in September 1993 to examine accountability and probity issues. The report of the task force, *Corporate Governance in the NHS*, made a number of recommendations. The taskforce set out to define corporate governance for the NHS and concluded that it consisted of the formulation of principles to guide the conduct of NHS organisations and individuals in the complex business of health care in the 1990s. These comprise:

- accountability, everything done by those who work in the NHS must be able to stand the test of parliamentary scrutiny, public judgment on propriety and professional codes of conduct.

- probity, there must be an absolute standard of honesty in dealing with assets in the NHS including integrity in personal conduct and in the use of information.

- openness, there should be transparency about NHS activities to promote confidence between the NHS, its patients and the public.

The taskforce's central recommendations were that:

- there should be an NHS Code of Conduct;

- a Code of Accountability for NHS boards should be adopted as the basis of delegation of functions from the Secretary of State, NHS authorities and trusts;

- clearer definitions of the functions of chairpersons and non-executive directors should be introduced and form the basis of appointment and induction processes, which must themselves be improved;

- a series of recommendations for ensuring financial control and probity were also made.

---

18 Public Accounts Committee 8th Report. *The Proper Conduct of Public Business* (HMSO, 1994).

It was also recommended that further work should be carried out on arrangements for identifying and appraising candidates for non-executive roles and the introduction of limits on the number of terms which could be served. They also suggested further work to define access to NHS information by the public, Community Health Councils, local government, voluntary and other local groups in the light of the government White Paper on *Open Government*.

The development of these Codes can be seen as one that is very much in line with new public management and the concept of corporate governance evident in the private sector.[19] The NHS taskforce defined corporate governance as consisting in the formulation of principles to guide the conduct of NHS organisations, namely accountability, probity and openness. The conceptual background of the codes is related to public service ethics and the codes are to a great extent reliant on the ethical behaviour of individuals. In taking this direction the taskforce has missed an opportunity to develop principles of good administrative practice. The Code of Accountability is intended to provide the basis of a new relationship between boards and the NHSE – 'a new informal contract' – but it does not create any statutory duties and the position of those who might be affected by a breach of the code is left unclear.[20] Although the codes include relatively detailed descriptions of the responsibilities of board members there is no indication or guidance on how non-executive board members are to carry out their function properly.

This is unfortunate, non-executive directors are intended to bring an element of independence to the operation of all NHS boards. Their perceptions and contributions can radically affect the quality of board performance. But research has found that their role varies enormously from board to board.[21] Variations were evident in the issues non executives were expected to address and in their involvement in ancillary matters outside routine board meetings. As a result the influence they brought to bear on board decisions also varied. This lack of consistency raises questions of board accountability and the legitimacy of the choices made. Members need guidance, information and good channels of communication to be able to function competently and improve accountability.

19 *Report of the Committee on the Financial Aspects of Corporate Governance* 'The Cadbury Report' (Dec 1992).

20 For detailed comment see Alice Belcher 'Codes of conduct and Accountability for NHS Boards' (1995) *Public Law* pp 288–297.

21 Charlotte Williams VC York Health Services Trust, 'Spice of Life' (1995) HSJ March.

The Corporate Governance Task Force did not directly address the issue of the appointment of chairpersons and non-executive directors to NHS boards. But plans to open up, to some extent, the process of appointment to NHS boards were announced in February 1995. There had been mounting criticism of current secretive procedures, including that voiced in evidence to the Nolan Inquiry into Standards in Public Life, and the fact that appointees were being drawn from too narrow a base. From April 1995, the process of appointment has to be better open to scrutiny and more accessible to people from a wider range of backgrounds, including women and ethnic minorities. Posts are advertised and those coming forward are considered against agreed selection criteria by 'independent' regional panels of chair persons and non executive directors. However the business orientation remains; candidates regarded as most likely to succeed will be those able to demonstrate 'critical detachment' and have experience of large scale organisation in the private business or public sector. It is hoped that this requirement will not take precedence over the need to demonstrate a close understanding of the local community and health service users.

Whilst the advertising of posts is to be welcomed, the process is still hardly open and fair in a constitutional sense. The Scottish and continental systems where persons from outside the public body are involved in the appointment of board chairs and non-executive members would be more democratic, but such procedures were rejected. Indeed it can be argued that boards should be politically balanced with some members appointed by local authorities and other bodies as well as being advertised to the general public as is the case in Canada. In no sense can health boards currently be said to be representative of the communities they serve. The revised method of appointment and a recent survey of the composition of board membership[22] tends to underline the continuation of the growth of the 'commercialisation' in the NHS.

MANAGEMENT REVIEW

In line with stated government policy to devolve as much decision-making as possible to a local level, the first Chief Executive of the NHSE stated that the flow of guidance to health authorities would be cut to an absolute minimum to allow an opportunity to develop a 'high quality, cost effective service suited to each districts needs'.[23] But

---

22 A recent survey found that 50% of local chairpersons were company directors, businessmen, accountants or management consultants.

23 D Nichol 'Strong hand with a Lighter Touch' (June 1989) HSJ.

despite the rhetoric of the 'hands off approach' the degree of direction and control exercised by the Executive over lower tiers of the NHS structure, through corporate contracts, and other means of review became much more detailed and extensive than had previously been the case. This is perhaps not entirely surprising. Such is the emphasis on economic efficiency that all levels of the NHS are under an obligation to deliver an efficient service within predetermined resources and consequently must monitor performance. In addition, the difficulties of planning and accountability that have marked successive health service re-organisations in the past, are still evident and the political pressure to minimise problems is considerable. The temptation to provide guidance and intervene at a prescriptive level is thus bound to be high.

Persistent criticism that bureaucracy was becoming overwhelming – 'a vast traffic of management coming from all directions' – and was constricting the potential of the reforms made it clear that the old management structure of the NHS was not entirely appropriate to the new pro-competitive, pro-market ethos.[24] At the end of 1993 the government outlined plans to restructure the management of the NHS. The proposals were the culmination of a struggle over the direction of the NHS in terms of the further development of its market activities and in effect tread a delicate line between giving hospital trusts more freedom on the one hand and retaining a firm grip at the centre on the other.[25] At the same time the provisions are likely to result in substantial savings in NHS central management.

The plans rejected calls to hive off the NHSE as a 'Next Steps' agency and instead resolved to keep it within the Department of Health and to develop further its function as the strategic rather than operational headquarters. The actual role and responsibilities of the Executive were left to be specifically defined in a later statement. The idea of dispensing with the intermediate regional tier of management between the Executive and Trusts and local health authorities was also dismissed. It was considered that the size, complexity and importance of the NHS was such that its central management needed to operate through a regional structure.

Instead, the paper proposed to replace all regional authorities and NHSE management 'outposts' to which Trusts were answerable with eight regional offices of the Executive which would oversee both the purchasing and provision of care. In this process some RHA functions were to be eliminated altogether, others were devolved to the local

---

24 *Unhealthy Competition* (Adam Smith Institute, 1994).
25 *Managing the New NHS* (Department of Health, 1993).

health authority level. In future, resource allocation for health authorities and GP fundholders would be handled by central management. Regional offices would be smaller than the current RHAs, but would ensure that purchasers had continued access to development activities. Clear criteria would be developed to define the circumstances in which central management could intervene to ensure that providers fulfilled their wider national policy objectives.

Each of the eight regional offices of the Executive are headed by a regional director and have a non executive representative on the NHS Policy Board to keep an eye on the interests of their area and to advise on appointments. The intention is that the functions of regional offices in relation to purchasers and providers are to be kept clear and distinct and regional managers will not become involved in detailed operational matters which are the responsibility of trusts and local health authorities.

It was also proposed to merge formally DHAs and Family Health Services Authorities (FHSAs) in order to establish one authority at local level which enable better integration of purchasing across the primary and secondary sectors and greater co-ordination of care. This action followed the recommendations of two Audit Commission reports which were published simultaneously[26] and which were critical of the persistence of traditional boundaries and the lack of any shared corporate strategy for the commissioning of health services. The current division limited any re-balancing of responsibility between general practices and health authorities. FHSAs were found to have only modest scope to co-ordinate the way general practice is evolving and DHAs had no formal links with general practices at all. These changes required new legislation which has been enacted in the Health Authorities Act (1995) which comes into force in April 1996.

Under this Act the Secretary of State for Health has a broad discretion to set up and abolish health authorities and decide how many there should be and who should serve on them. Health authorities and FHSAs are authorised to move towards merger by carrying out one anothers functions from the period of Royal Assent to 1 April 1996. This reorganisation is unlikely to be as disruptive as might appear at first sight, as many of the changes have been taking place within the existing statutory framework. In a number of areas district and FHSAs have already merged and the Health Authorities Act (1995) (to be referred to as the 1995 Act) merely formalises and legitimises these arrangements. An amendment to the 1995 Act to

---

26 *Practice Makes Perfect: the role of the Family Health Services Authority* (Audit Commission Report, No 10) and *Their Business, Your Health: the new role of the District Health Authority* (Audit Commission Report, HMSO 1993, No 11).

make health authorities coterminous with local authority boundaries where practicable was rejected. A bid to include nurses and doctors on health boards also fell, but GPs will in future be able to be members.

At the time of writing there is a three month period of consultation in operation over the new health authority boundaries. Chairs and non-executive directors will be appointed during the autumn of 1995. In many parts of the country where health authorities and FHSAs have already merged in all but the technical legal sense consultation will tend to be academic. All that remains to resolved will be board appointments and it is certain that the opportunity will be taken to 'weed out' non-executive directors who are not now politically acceptable. But the 1995 Act will not bring about any single model for purchasing. The changes have been driven by the bottom up and set by the activities of purchasing and the different models that have emerged to meet the needs of different localities and which will remain. At the same time it is clear that the government has a preference for fundholding as the model of commissioning. This is being emphasised and encouraged by health authorities, such that April 1996 is yet one more step in health service reform rather than the end of the road.

The proposals received a mixed reception amid criticism that the future roles of regional offices and health authorities were far from clear and disappointment that the Department of Health and the Executive had escaped relatively unscathed; regions bearing the brunt of the changes. There were also concerns that the abolition of RHAs would render public accountability even more elusive. In April 1994 the number of RHAs was reduced from 14 to eight and they were divested of their previous functions in preparation for the formal legislative restructuring the following year. The eight remaining RHAs set up a joint management structure with the regional offices of the NHSE which took over the non statutory functions of the RHAs. From the 1 April 1996 these eight offices will be all that remains of the former regional tier of the NHS hierarchy. Appointment of officers of these regional outposts of the NHME is to be decided by the NHSE itself not by regulation. In effect these officers will be civil servants, their function will be to advise Ministers. Accordingly they will be governed by the Armstrong Code and any subsequent amendments or developments.[27]

Once the proposals had been announced, 12 function groups began to develop a framework for the future organisation of the NHS. Managing the new NHS: Functions and Responsibilities in the New

---

27 The Treasury and Civil Service Committee recently recommended the establishment of a Civil Service Code.

NHS set out to clarify the roles and responsibilities of each part of the organisation.[28] The work of the groups was said to be guided by four key principles; meeting the requirements of parliamentary and public accountability; devolving responsibility to local level; developing a single corporate structure for central management; and simplifying and streamlining management arrangements, although the latter two seem to have been given primacy at the expense of the two former. The core functions of the new health authorities will be to evaluate the health and health care needs of the local population, establish a strategy to meet those needs within national priorities and implement that strategy by purchasing the necessary services. There is new provision relating to health authority arrangements for seeking advice from health professionals to enable their functions to be performed effectively.[29] Health authorities are under a duty to seek advice, but this new section and the consequent guidance issued by the NHSE leaves a great deal of discretion to health authorities as to its source and the means by which it is obtained.

Regional NHSE office functions will include performance management of RHAs, monitoring of NHS Trust performance that cannot be readily provided for through the contracting process, advising on and approving capital investment by Trusts and ensuring that the NHS market operates effectively.

Running alongside the group activities mentioned above was the Banks Review of the Department of Health. Banks noted that whilst ever there was a publicly funded service which provided the bulk of care to almost the entire population there was always going to be a tension between the drive for decentralisation and the legitimate requirements for effective accountability. The NHSE in effect faced two directions; as the top tier of the NHS it needed to be culturally close to the service; and at the same time it was unequivocally part of government, responsible for implementing government policies and holding the NHS to account. The real challenge was to manage these tensions, so that health authorities and trusts were in the driving seat, but within a focused strategy set by ministers who could confidently and legitimately defend the overall performance of the NHS.

In order to manage this the Department of Health has undergone an internal shake up but no policy areas have actually been discarded. Three main areas of 'business' have been allocated for the development of policy; the NHSE, social care and public health. The NHSE has been

---

28 (NHSE, July 1994). See also *Statement of Responsibilities and Accountabilities: public health, the NHS and social care* (Department of Health, May 1995).

29 Schedule 1, para 3 and 'Ensuring Involvement of Professionals in Health Authority Work' (HSG (95))11.

given responsibility for overseeing all stages of health services from policy development through implementation, to monitoring and review.

The criticism has been made that Banks failed to grasp the opportunity for adequate pruning because she was part of the civil service culture and did not truly understand the dynamics of relationships within the Department of Health. She was consequently accused of 're-arranging the cutlery without looking at the menu'.[30] Whether these latest changes will result in less intervention in health authority and trust activity remains to be seen, much depends on the attitude of the Secretary of State for Health and whether the temptation to prescribe can be overcome by the central management.

The establishment of regional offices of the NHSE is of course meant to shift the centre of gravity of the NHSE nearer the service. But the threat of centralisation is likely to remain strong as there few ground rules evident in the current reviews for guiding or regulating the relationship between purchasers and providers. To some extent a number of the concerns expressed at the time that proposals to restructure were announced have already been borne out. A recent survey amongst health services managers found that the strategic direction of health services was unclear and there was a feeling that the newly formed regional offices were too remote and out of touch; not only less independent of the Department of Health than before but also more heavy-handed.[31] The general consensus was that there now needed to be a period of stability and consolidation in health service organisation to allow for the opportunity for public service values to be reasserted.

Despite the number of reviews and publishing of Codes, as currently constituted the NHS still displays an over-concentration of public accountability through a single point, the Secretary of State. This is neither adequate nor reasonable. Local health bodies are daily making decisions about local needs and priorities. Indeed a key element of the reformed health service is that local purchasers make local choices. Accountability at a local level is thus needed for such actions. Proper accountability requires rather more than the invocation of codes of practice, it requires a means of holding to account and the giving of an account. Improved codes of practice and openness are welcome in that they contribute to the latter but do little to address the former. If local people do not like what is being done there are no

---

30 (HSJ, 11 August 1994) p 5.
31 (HSJ, January 1995).

means for them to remove those responsible.[32] The contrast with local government is marked. Local authorities as well as being subject to electoral accountability are also subject to a wide range of provisions to ensure their activities are open to public scrutiny and external monitoring. The recent spate of task forces, reviews and committees has done nothing to address this central democratic deficit of the NHS.

GENERAL PRACTICE

Since its inception a prominent feature of the NHS has been the separation of general practice from hospital services. General practitioners (GPs) in the UK are independent contractors who derive their income from a blend of various forms of payment. They operate a primary care service and some 90% of general practice consultations are dealt with entirely within the practice. The remaining percentage are referred to hospital for further investigation, a second opinion or treatment. The GP therefore carries out what is commonly referred to as a 'gatekeeper function' in relation to acute services and has held a key role in controlling access to hospital services and use of resources.

The responsibility for the planning and management of GP services has been that of the FHSA. As a result of the 1990 re-organisation FHSAs were given a number of additional tasks. These included oversight of the introduction of indicative prescribing amounts for GPs, GP practice budgets, medical audit, and the development of information technology to assist the monitoring of GP prescribing and referral rates. As a consequence of its extended role certain changes were also made to FHSA structure, management and line of accountability.

The size of FHSAs was slimmed down and general managers were appointed to be responsible for the management of administrative business and the implementation of new FHSA responsibilities. Instead of being directly accountable to the Department of Health as was previously the case, FHSAs were made accountable to the relevant RHA which allocated FHSA funds, reviewed performance and monitored their plans, which were required to be co-ordinated with those of the DHAs. This change in the line of accountability of FHSAs was a move which was generally welcomed as it was hoped it would lead to better strategic integration of primary health care and hospital services. In order to discharge responsibilities with the degree of flexibility necessary for different areas FHSAs were freed to determine

---

32 Howard Davis and Guy Daly, 'Codes of Conduct are not Enough' (1995) *IHSM Network* Vol 2, 4.

their own sub-committee structures, with the exception of those committees which dealt with complaints about GPs who were allegedly in breach of their contract, and the Medical Audit Advisory Committee.

In April 1990 the government also introduced a new contract for GPs, although in essence this was more a modification of the old one than any real innovation. The new contract aimed to influence both the quality of care and costs. In line with the general ideology to stimulate 'consumerism' in the provision of health care there was a small but significant change in the way doctors pay was calculated, in that capitation pay was increased and the basic practice allowance decreased. There were also a number of measures which sought to relate financial awards to the quality of care: the use of deputising services was discouraged through the introduction of differential pay for call out during unsocial hours; targets were set for some preventive measures such as childhood immunisations and cervical cytology; payments are also now made for medical checks carried out on all new patients and those over 75 years of age. Finally any patients suffering from a chronic condition also attract additional payment.

FUND HOLDING

One of the more radical changes to health service provision has been the introduction of practice budgets or fundholding for GPs. These measures were seen by government to provide an opportunity to improve the quality of services by stimulating competition for patients not only between GPs, but competition for contracts between general practices and DHAs.

Gradually the size of practices or groups of practices able to apply for budgets has been brought down so that those with as few as 5,000 patients are now entitled to purchase a defined range of hospital services such as outpatients services, diagnostic tests and some in-patient and day-case treatments. Budgets also include allowances for practice costs, staff, premises and drugs. The element of the budget concerned with hospital services is deducted from the allocation of the relevant local health authority. A current, upper limit of £6,000 has been placed on the cost of hospital treatment which a practice has to meet from its own budget for any individual patient. Perhaps surprisingly, RHAs rather than FHSAs were made responsible for considering applications for funding and for determining the size of GP fund-holder budgets, despite the latter being required to be involved in the budget setting process because of their detailed local knowledge. The reason given by government for this move was that

FHSAs were considered to be too close to the practitioners in their area. The provision did however to some extent maintain the philosophy of the separation of funding and provision, evident throughout other sectors of the service.

One of the main, initial criticisms of the fundholding provisions was that public confidence in GPs might be undermined and the patient-doctor relationship distorted if financial considerations had to be taken into account in clinical decisions. The concern was that budgets may place doctors in the unwelcome position of having to seek savings from patient medical care to fund other developments in their practices and consequently may avoid taking on relatively costly patients such as the elderly or those experiencing chronic illness. When questioned on this point by the Social Services Select Committee the Secretary of State replied that this would not be allowed to happen since specific local needs of patients would be taken into account when practice budgets were set.[33]

However this may have been insufficient to reduce the risks of funded practices favouring healthy patients. There has been evidence to suggest that some GPs are unwilling to take on patients with a chronic condition which requires continual prescribing, although the incidence has not been as great as was once feared.[34]

Other criticisms focused on the efficacy of operating practice budgets. The patient population of most GPs was regarded by some commentators to be too low to make allowances for the risk of high cost incidents without distorting available resources. Enthoven had suggested that a viable patient population, one that could absorb risk, would be between 50–100,000 patients.[35] In addition it was feared that there might be a lack of the managerial skills and information technology necessary to run budgets effectively. Not only were information systems either absent from most general practices or inadequate for the enlarged tasks of fund holding, but health care providers themselves did not generally have sufficiently detailed data available to enable GPs to make informed judgments about the quality and costs of the care which they would purchase. Although DHAs compiled information packs for commissioning GPs, these tended only to set out broad quality principles, list available services and indicate the number of patients treated in each speciality.

Marinker pointed out however that many of the criticisms levelled at fundholding practices had previously been made about

---

33   8th Report; 19.

34   D Longley, *Health Service Complaints* (ESRC, 1992).

35   A Enthoven, 'Words from the Source' (1989) BMJ NHS *Review* 1167.

contemporary general practice. He argued that many aspects of fundholding were extensions and elaboration of current practice. What was new, and giving rise to concern, was the scale and speed at which change was being encouraged to take place.[36] There appeared to be few safeguards within the process to ensure that patients would benefit individually or that GPs would be accountable to the public for the operation of practices and the services provided, other than in relation to expenditure.

All fundholding practices have to produce an annual report and the accounts of practice budgets are audited by the Audit Commission as part of its audit of health bodies. Regulations have been made which specify the categories of valid expenditure and also how surpluses may be spent. These are supplemented as necessary by detailed guidance. Even though there is no intention that surpluses should boost the individual income of doctors it is very difficult to prove that this has not in fact occurred.

Further means to contain costs in general practice were introduced through the use of allocated indicative amounts for drugs. Expenditure on drugs is the largest single element of family health services spending and an attempt to control wasteful and unnecessarily expensive prescribing was initiated by what was known as the Selected List in the 1980s. The newer arrangements are intended to place 'a downward pressure on expenditure on drugs'. Indicative drug amounts, which include appliances, dressings and chemical reagents are based on the average for practices in the area and are intended to encourage prescribing of generic drugs instead of expensive alternatives. The intention is also to discourage any prescribing at all where the benefit to patients would only be marginal.

General practitioners have argued that the use of indicative drug amounts has led to a loss of choice and clinical freedom to prescribe and have pointed out that the cost of medication should be viewed in terms of quality, effectiveness and efficiency. Older generic drugs may be less effective than continually developed, branded ones and may carry considerable side effects which affect the quality of a patient's well-being. These factors have long term implications for the totality of costs for health care which should be carefully monitored so that open, appropriate standards for quality, not just monetary costs, can be ascertained.[37]

36   Bevan and Marinker *Greening the White Paper; a Strategy for NHS Reform* (Social Market Foundation, 1989) pp 27–34.

37   Bevan and Marinker *ibid* pp 13, 14.

Since the first, somewhat hesitant steps were taken towards fundholding in 1990 the face of general practice has changed considerably. By 1993 the number of practice managers had increased by 43%, practice nurses by over 50% and computer operators by 300%. GPs are being encouraged to take on not only more tasks but differing roles. General practice is consequently diversifying, developing rapidly from GPs working alone or within a small group of colleagues to organisations providing community based health services.

Two government papers spell out the thrust of the future developments[38] and encourage GPs to be increasingly involved in commissioning secondary care either as fundholders or alternatively as members of commissioning groups which advise local health authorities. This is seen as strengthening the agency role of general practice in which the family doctor acts as agent for the patient and has a potential to improve the quality of secondary care.

The British Medical Association (BMA) has also put GPs at the heart of the NHS as either fundholders, members of locality purchasing consortia or as a major presence on health boards. The BMA has gone so far as to propose that NHS Trusts be scrapped and responsibility for all secondary care be given to GPs.[39]

But the Institute of Health Service Management (IHSM) has been critical of the failure of the government to ensure that GPs are properly accountable and has claimed that misuse of fundholding savings amounts to some £120m. Despite government response to these concerns[40] accountability to some extent remains confused. Fundholders are statutorily accountable to the NHSE regional offices which will arbitrate disputes, but their day to day contact is with the new health authorities with whom local strategies are decided.

It is also argued that the sanction of expulsion from fundholding status for breaches of GP accountability is ineffective because resources are already committed before action can be taken. In addition there is uncertainty about whether the purchasing decisions of fundholding GPs fall within breach of terms of service for the purpose of patient complaints. Thus it is not entirely evident how purchasing fundholders are accountable to the public and there needs to be clarification of to whom patients should address grievances.

---

38 *Developing NHS Purchasing and GP Fundholding* (EL(94) 79 NHSE, 1994) and Developing *NHS Fundholding; towards a primary care-led NHS* (NHSE, 1994).

39 *Future Models for the NHS; a discussion paper* (Health Policy and Economic Research Unit, BMA, 1994).

40 *An Accountability Framework for GP Fundholders* (March 1995).

Whilst initially fundholding was regarded as the 'wild card' in the pack of health service reforms, GPs themselves are increasingly experimenting with different kinds of packages including the formation of fundholding consortia. These are relatively loose alliances where practices are able to opt in or out of initiatives, but are able to pool expertise, and reduce workloads for both GPs and Trusts.[41]

Total fundholding, the buying all health and community care services is also being developed through a small number of national pilots. There are few central regulations relevant to these and the projects are creating their own rules, whilst attempting to remain within central guidelines. The Trusts involved in these developments are deemed to have benefited from extra resources and from the lessening of the complexity of dealing with individual fundholders. Both providers and health authorities are full members of the project boards which set strategy and direction, but the purchasing forum comprises only of GPs and the health authority. It has been argued that such projects provide a more focused debate over difficult purchasing issues as GPs are more likely to have a clear view of what is needed for their patients and of the strengths and weaknesses of local providers. It is also argued that they are more able than health authorities to spur improvements by real or implied shifts of resources from local providers.[42] However, others prefer to support the development of primary care health agencies which would provide holistic community based services. However, no single model may be ideal in all situations and it is therefore necessary to consider experimentation and diversity within a strong framework of national objectives.[43]

However the transition of GPs to key players in the new health service is not without cost. The extension of GP fundholding and push towards a primary care-led health service has left many GPs uncertain of their role, and dissatisfied with both the administrative and clinical overload. Ironically, GPs are being placed in the position of being both purchasers and providers of services which reverses one of the primary tenets of the reforms. Many feel that the fundamental values of general practice are in danger of being eroded, if that is not already the case.[44]

Others are questioning the rising cost of management and administration. The marginal costs of GP fundholding maybe three

41 See, eg, The Berkshire Integrated Purchasing Project which comprises six fundholding practices and the health authority jointly managing services for 85,000 patients. This comes close to the recommendations of Enthoven.

42 'Room at the top; total fundholding' (HSJ November, 1994).

43 *Primary health care; a prognosis* (IPPR).

44 P Gordon, 'Core Values' (March 1995) HSJ.

times higher than the cost of health authority purchasing.[45] This is creating a layer of bureaucracy which is fundholder led but which, in effect, is generating what are substantially health authorities in all but name. The National Association of Commissioning GPs, an organisation of non-fundholding GPs points out that they offer collectively more time and expertise to the contracting process whilst minimising the impact on the clinical workload. This has the advantage of low management costs and quality secondary care which is equitably available to all patients, preventing the development of a two tier service and the concern that fundholding undermines the principle of equity and results in differential resources and waiting times.

As the number of small fundholders rises so does the cost for trusts negotiating with them. On the other hand, if total fundholding were to become a reality trusts should be able to negotiate larger and more strategic deals. In this way the strengths of GP fundholding – decisions made by clinicians close to the patient might be preserved and the prime weakness, namely excessive fragmentation might be reduced. But, the fundamental question still remains as to local consumer representation in these crucial decision-making processes.

The vision of primary led care is nothing new, but for many years secondary care has attracted the major share of health service resources, not to mention public attention. Acute care has come to be identified with technical progress and 'serious' treatment. Primary care has to a large extent been made the Cinderella of the health service, a 'weak aspiration seeking to become a core concept'.[46] To attain its potential primary care needs strong strategy to support it. Family doctors have taken the lead in practice investment and in providing a wider range of local services. There is a potential for new kinds of home based care and innovation, as conditions now appear to favour local incentives and enterprise. But GPs must be seen to deliver effective services to key patient groups and show a capacity to respond to serious life threatening illnesses as acceptance of changes entails shared care and joint ventures, an emphasis on planning and organisation, not to mention a sea change in public perception.

Hospital consultants as well as GPs have generally welcomed the opportunity to provide certain secondary care services in the primary care setting. But concerns have been expressed that the quality of services may suffer, not through any lack of technical expertise, but

---

45 6% of budgets compared with 1.7% of health authority costs.
46 N Bosanquet, 'Reviving Sleeping Beauty' (April 1995) HSJ.

through lack of experience in diagnostic interpretation and in relating symptoms to alternative diagnosis. Quality and costs thus need to be monitored carefully to ensure provision of efficient and effective services.

By April 1996 GPs with only 5,000 patients will be allowed to join fundholding which will also be extended to cover elective surgery, (other than a few rare and high cost exceptions), most outpatient attendances and a wide range of community health services. In addition a new 'easy entry' community fundholding scheme will open to practices with as few as 3,000 patients and cover drugs, diagnostic tests and community health services. Total purchasing is also to be extended. Whilst fundholding theoretically remains voluntary rather than compulsory, circumstances may push all GPs, however reluctant to the forefront of health service provision in one way or another.

As GP purchasing increases in one form or another the newly merged health authorities will have differing relationships with a wide range of groups and will gradually lose their community role. Except for areas of public health they will act increasingly as regulators, monitoring the quality of services purchased. How will distant regulators, without elected members, ensure recognition of local voices? This brings us back to the point that in the health care market the purchasers are not users and there is a triangular relationship. All three corners, purchasers, providers and users must be put under a statutory duty to consult one another. Unless this is formalised and embedded in the system it will be a matter of chance whether the public does well or badly out of extended fundholding and regulatory health authorities.[47]

THE ROLE OF CONTRACT IN THE NHS

As in New Zealand, the pivot of the new health service since 1991 is the imposed use of contract as the vehicle which underpins the implementation of policy and provision of services. The contract mechanism is regarded as having two main advantages. It separates the role and responsibilities of purchasers from providers and by formally setting out criteria and targets for delivery and it provides a means of focusing both purchaser and provider attention on the quality of health care and supplying a catalyst for improvement. The purported intention is that accountability will be enhanced through the network of contractual obligations negotiated between the parties. This

---

47   J Neuberger (November 1994) HSJ.

could provide an opportunity to develop health care which reflects community needs and preferences and for monitoring to be placed in a wider context which includes procedures for feedback from GPs and patients themselves.

However, in order to realise the potential of informed contracting the respective roles of medical professionals, managers and the public have to undergo some reappraisal. In particular the challenge is to avoid using inappropriate 'shopping lists' and instead develop frameworks which are able to recognise and balance the disparate values and interests within a community.

In English law there is no general concept of the public law or administrative contract as a means of governing relationships between government and the private sector, or between different parts of the public sector. Consequently a variety of contractual means are at the disposal of purchasers, each of which is subject to a different dispute resolution procedure. Genuine contracts, which give rise to traditional rights and obligations and which are governed by private law, continue to be made between the public and private health care sectors. Alongside these conventional contracts a system of 'NHS contracts' operates[48] which provides the legal mechanism for the provision of services between parties within the NHS. The NHS contract is the only special legal regime to have been created by legislation.

Section 4 (3) of the 1990 Act provides that an NHS contract:

> shall not be regarded for any purpose as giving rise to contractual rights or liabilities, but if any dispute arises with respect to such an arrangement, either party may refer the matter to the Secretary of State for determination ...

In fact, the Secretary of State carries very wide powers in relation to the process of contracting. These unusually extend to the pre-contractual stage as s 4(4) of the 1990 Act provides:

> If in the course of negotiations intending to lead to an arrangement which will be an NHS contract, it appears to the health service body
>
> (a) that the terms proposed by another health service body are unfair by reason that the other is seeking to take advantage of its position as the only, or the only practicable, provider of the goods or services concerned or by reason of any other unequal bargaining position as between the prospective parties to the proposed arrangement; or
>
> (b) that for any reason arising out of the relative bargaining position of the prospective parties any of the terms of the proposed arrangements cannot be agreed;

---

48   1990 Act s 4.

that health service body may refer the terms of the proposed arrangement to the Secretary of State for determination ...

Once a reference has been made, the Secretary of State may then write the contract for the parties and order them to proceed with it. The availability of this procedure creates a situation radically different from that of private law contract. Once contract negotiations have begun, neither party can withdraw without the permission of the other or of the Secretary of State.

As regards existing NHS contracts adjudication by the Secretary of State (or adjudicator, if one is appointed) may contain such directions as he considers appropriate to resolve the dispute. He may vary the terms of the NHS contract, or bring it to an end. Any such variation or termination is to be treated as being put in effect by the parties. He may also give such directions as he considers appropriate in order to give satisfactory effect to the variation or termination.

Guidance issued on resolving disputes states that all NHS contracts should be constructed so as to minimise the risk of dispute and should include clauses for agreed arbitration if either party believes that a contract has been broken.[49] The parties to the contract should specify an arbitrator, who will usually be a regional officer, but there are no obstacles to them agreeing to private arbitration. They may also agree the terms on which arbitration may take place. Where disputes arise over the terms of a proposed contract guidance states that the parties are expected to seek the assistance of a regional officer as conciliator, in order to obtain an impartial view of the proposed terms.

These arrangements do not alter the right of either party to invoke the formal dispute resolution procedure provided by the 1990 Act. However the view of the NHSE is that 'informal' arrangements, supported by a shared objective of securing effective health services should reduce the need to use the statutory dispute resolution process.[50]

In reality enforcement of contracts appears to be much less of a clear cut process than was anticipated. There is evidence to suggest that the model of arbitration chosen for the NHS contract disputes is an inappropriate mechanism for dealing with disputes arising at the pre-contract stage. These are the kind of dispute that are most frequently emerging and they mostly concern pricing and activity levels. Widely differing approaches are taken by regions to the resolution of disputes

---

49   NHS contracts; guidance on resolving disputes. NHS management executive EL(91)11.

50   For an examination of dispute resolution procedures in practice see I Harden and D Longley 'NHS Contracts' (1994) in Termination of Contracts (Birds, Bradgate and Villiers eds, Wiley Chancery).

but the distinction between arbitration and conciliation which is set out in the NHSE guidance is largely neglected so that the same mechanisms are applied to both pre contract and contract disputes.[51] Furthermore, the pricing and activity level disagreements are frequently bound up with long-standing issues of service restructuring and funding. Consequently 'many strategic planning issues that are not resolved elsewhere are washed up on the shore of contracting'.[52] The informal dispute processes used are not geared to the resolution of such complex issues, particularly as the system often used in the NHS includes pendulum decisions where the adjudicator must find for one side or the other and cannot compromise. Hopefully, the present reorganisation of the regional tier of the NHS will provide the opportunity to promote review of the efficacy of current procedures for the settling of contract disputes as a whole and at the least promote improvement and consistency throughout the process.

Whilst the clear intention of the 1990 Act is to preclude the possibility of litigation in relation to rights and liabilities that might otherwise arise between the parties, were NHS contracts to be subject to private law, it is arguable that this would not exclude an application for judicial review in some circumstances. Notwithstanding the issue of privity of contract in English law it is feasible that the content of contractual agreements might give rise to a legitimate expectation of a defined quality or quantity services for the consumer. In the past applications for judicial review to provide specific services have not been successful because of lack of any definition of what is actually to be provided. Where provision is articulated in a contract or set out as a standard in a charter, the courts might be prepared to lend support that a legitimate expectation of a certain provision or quality of service has arisen. However is difficult to envisage the precise circumstances in which this kind of argument might succeed, given recent judgments on the doctrine of legitimate expectation and the distinction drawn between procedural and substantive requirements.

Although contracts are generally made on a three year rolling basis, formal review is necessary each year as health authorities receive their funding annually. Review therefore considers possible changes in service specifications arising from any alterations in resources or priorities. In terms of accountability contracting activities are very much an uncharted area. The Department of Health has emphasised the importance of monitoring the quality of service provision and a

---

51   *ibid.*
52   D Hughes, L Griffiths and J McHale, 'Whose Problem?' (April 1995) HSJ.

critical issue in the contracting process is the setting of standards which meet the requirements of the purchaser and which the provider has an obligation to meet.

The National Audit Office found that health authorities suffered from a lack of information, a lack of consultation with clinicians and too little of innovation of contract types.[53] The difficulties and complexity of the contract process was also underlined by the Audit Commission in their review of the role of DHAs.[54] It found that contracting was often hampered by a shortage of information, health authority personnel skills and a lack of clarity about the process. To improve the ability of contracts to actually influence service provision health authorities needed to encourage the development of clinical guidelines and auditing of compliance with them, define and monitor a limited number of realistic and measurable quality targets and develop pricing arrangements which actually influenced providers to deliver the required quality and quantity of activity.

EXTRA-CONTRACTUAL REFERRALS

Whilst most patients receive health services under contract, a number of referrals will inevitably not be included in NHS contracts and must be paid for separately. Such referrals are known as extra-contractual referrals (ECRs) and were originally intended to provide a safety net to cover gaps in services on the premise that money would follow the patient. ECRs thus tend to cover a miscellaneous and shifting collection of services which fall outside contracts for varying reasons.

Purchasers require notice of ECRs other than those which arise as a result of an emergency and may refuse authorisation or payment if notice is not given. However, the NHSE advises that is it unacceptable to for a purchaser to refuse authorisation solely on the grounds of the proposed cost. Legitimate invoices relating to emergency ECRs on the other hand have to be settled unconditionally, as do tertiary referrals from consultants.[55]

By their nature ECRs are largely unpredictable and their management is a complex task requiring a balancing of factors. The system creates something of a dilemma for health authorities because on the one hand they need to respect choice for patients as far as is possible, on the other they must aim to keep expenditure within

53 *Contracting for Acute Health Care* (NAO HMSO, 1994).
54 *Their Health Your Business* (Audit Commission HMSO, 1993).
55 (1993) NHSE EL (92) 97.

prescribed limits. In general there has been an increase in emergency ECRs, the volume of elective ECRs and very high cost ECRs where there tends to be limited knowledge of effectiveness.[56] But amongst health authorities the amount of overspending on ECRs or the percentage ECR budget of overall spending varies enormously. In addition, what constitutes an ECR or a contracted service tends to be arbitrary, depending on the location of the providers and the types of service provided in each individual health authority. Unlike the position in New Zealand there is no equivalent in the NHS to the Core Services Committee[57] and no attempt has been made to define core services.

The Audit Commission recommended that all health authorities should have an explicit policy on ECRs which explains the circumstances in which requests may be redirected, delayed or deferred. But not all health authorities have written, widely disseminated ECR policies and increasingly, in an effort to keep within their budget, health authorities are specifying exclusions from ECRs. These have included procedures for in vitro fertilisation, AIDS related ECRs, cosmetic surgery, homeopathy, residential drug and alcohol dependency treatment. Other health authorities prefer to operate a more flexible arrangement for ECRs through the use of waiting lists.

Maheswaran has argued that precisely because of their safety net role ECRs have become an administrative burden and a repository for all the anomalies thrown up by the implementation of the internal market. Adoption of an ECR policy alone will not curb overspending.[58] Consequently, health authorities need clear guidelines at regional or national level to help them make difficult choices. But if this is to include adequate public choice the development of ECR policy also needs input from the local population and practitioners as well as public health specialists.

MARKET TESTING

In addition to the NHS contracting process the concept of market testing is regarded by the government as having a significant role to play in improving service delivery and promoting value for money.[59] Guidance issued recently by NHSE sets out to encourage the extension

---

56   S Auplish and E Shires 'Who Goes Where?' (September 1994) HSJ.

57   See Chapter 3 pp 90–4.

58   S Maheswaran 'Heavy weight' (November 1994) HSJ.

59   *Competing for Quality* (NHSE, 1991).

of the market testing to clinical and clinical support services. The guidance also instructs Trusts which have not already done so to market test all catering, laundry and domestic services by March 1996 and warns that managerial performance will be judged partly on progress in meeting this target.

However, there is empirical evidence[60] to suggest that whilst many Trust managers consider the market testing process to have some merit, it is not only time consuming but any benefit gained may be offset by the cost of current evaluation procedures. As a result, scarce resources may be being diverted into unprofitable procedures for the sake of political ideology. The research found that management was prepared to use market testing as a tool to improve quality efficiency and value in certain selected circumstances but that the process had failed to meet the expectations of both clients and contractors. Consequently, contracting out had, as yet, made little penetration into the NHS and it was unlikely that it could ever be accepted as the prime means to raise standards. If the ultimate goal of the NHSE is to proceed with the market testing of clinical services there appears to be some way to go to convince Trusts of the efficacy of the move, unless a more efficient and less time consuming process is evolved.

Perhaps mention should be made at this point of the Private Finance Initiative (PFI) the aim of which is to provide new facilities for the NHS in a cost effective way, transferring the certain risks inherent in projects to the private sector. The intention is that services provided by the private sector remain firmly in the overall control of Trusts but the involvement of private sector finance frees up more resources for Trusts to use for patient care.[61] However, some private enterprises appear to be re-thinking their ambitions to provide core NHS clinical services because of the increasing number of initiatives won by in-house teams. There is a perceived reluctance by the private sector to take on the degree of risk involved in NHS initiatives without being able to charge sufficiently for doing so. This is not surprising, as the outlay can be considerable but the commitments are only short term.

CHOICE AND PUBLIC PARTICIPATION IN HEALTH CARE POLICY

As the structure of the National Health Service in recent years has become increasingly concerned with management review and

---

60   D Decker, 'Market Testing – does it bring home the bacon?' (Jan 1995) HSJ.
61   Department of Health 95/430.

accountability for expenditure, dissatisfaction has often been expressed, despite the role of Community Health Councils, with the consistent failure to foster measures for a wider concept of public accountability which facilitates adequate consumer input and representation.

Community Health Councils (CHC) were established in 1974 and are under a broadly defined statutory duty to represent the public in their district.[62] Although CHCs have been criticised for not being generally representative of the local community because of the preponderance of members from the professional sections of society, they do go some way to providing a systematic element of public involvement in health matters at a local level. About half of the 18–24 members are nominated by the local authority, a third by local voluntary organisations and the remainder by Region. Each CHC has a Chair and Vice Chair chosen by the members and a small, remunerated support staff.

Recently, CHCs have expressed concern about 'creeping commercialism' and alarm that they may be funded according to performance related criteria under NHSE proposals. The Association of Community Health Councils in England and Wales (ACHCEW) is concerned about the level of service and support CHCs will receive once regional offices of the NHSE have replaced RHAs as the establishing bodies for CHCs. The NHSE has proposed to establish a range and volume of core CHC work that a minimum of two staff might be expected to carry out. ACHCEW has also raised objections to proposals to centre management of CHC recruitment, pay and contracts with just one health authority per region. This they point out has potential implications for the independence of CHCs in the area of the selected health authority.[63]

Unfortunately there has always been a lack of guidance on how Community Health Councils should fulfil their function and each Council has had to interpret and negotiate its own working relationship, not only with its local health authority but with other institutions concerned with health care and with the consumers CHCs are designated to represent. Not unlike the situation relating to non executive members of NHS boards, this has inevitably resulted in some diversity of CHC involvement and effectiveness in local planning.[64]

---

62   NHS Act (1977) Schedule 7 and CHC Regs (1985).

63   (February 1995) HSJ.

64   Klein and Lewis, *The Politics of Consumer Representation; A study of CHCs* (1976) Centre for Studies in Social Policy: 124-126.

Although under the 1990 re-organisation the statutory duties of CHCs have remained unaltered subsequent guidance has introduced a number of key changes which have affected CHC involvement in local health planning.[65] Community Health Councils have a right to be consulted by the relevant health authority when a substantial development or variation in services is contemplated. But there are no formal provisions for Community Health Councils to be consulted on health care issues on a wider, regional or national basis although some RHAs did, on occasion, involve CHCs in strategic planning and the Association of Community Health Councils in England and Wales (ACHCEW) regularly considers and submits responses to national policy documents to the Department of Health and the NHSE.[66]

On the face of it, the statutory provision for consultation and indeed Department of Health emphasis on 'involving the consumer' suggests that there is an underlying intention that decisions should be subject to open and reasoned debate, enabling differing interests be taken into account before policy has actually become consolidated. Consultation procedures thus imply a commitment to public input and choice. This is certainly the impression given by the new Code of Conduct and Accountability which recommends that 'NHS Trusts and authorities should forge an open relationship with the local community and should conduct a dialogue about the service provided. NHS organisations should demonstrate to the public that they are concerned with the wider health of the population'. This also suggests that coherent and defensible reasons for action or non action will be put forward.

In practice consultation since the 1990 reforms has become essentially 'deregulated'. Statutory provisions do not now sit well with the revised NHS structure and ethos. This is because the *duty* to consult does not extend to Trusts who have largely taken over from health authorities as the prime instigators of variations in services. In effect, communication and consultation relies on the triangular relationship between the CHC and purchasers and providers. This can result in a process of exclusion rather than inclusion because of differential access to information and resources which enable preferred groups to set agendas and the terms of debate before any formal consultation process begins.[67] The process of consultation, if not carefully structured and monitored, may therefore simply perform a legitimising function rather than provide a channel for any real contribution to decision-making.

---

65   (EL (90) 185).

66   C Hogg *The Public and the NHS* (ACHCEW, 1986).

67   I Harden and N Lewis (1986) *op cit.*

Several criticisms of CHC consultation procedures in particular and health service consultation provision generally can be made on this account. The process of consultation in relation to a variation in services is generally two staged. Initially there is a period of informal consultation on tentative, though often well advanced proposals. Generally this amounts to a no more than a definition of the issues by exchange of letters or low-key discussion at an informal meeting. There then follows a short period of formal consultation in which comments are invited within three months. It is suggested in Department of Health guidelines that the consultation document should set out, amongst other things, the reasons for change, the relationship with other development plans and implications for patients. The guidelines envisage that where sufficient local agreement exists it should be possible to move from proposal to actual implementation within six months.[68] However there is no requirement for the health authority to publish its response to any CHC comment or to give reasons for rejection of any proposals put forward by the CHC.

CHCs have never been empowered to enforce any recommendations they might make and could only veto proposed changes in service provision if able to put forward a viable alternative that was accepted by the health authority concerned. When responding to consultation CHCs are not required to submit any counter proposal, but a frequent complaint of health councils remains that they receive insufficient information about proposed changes, making both rational comment and the task of even suggesting any acceptable alternatives extremely difficult.

Temporary or phased changes in provision generally lie outside the above procedures and some health authorities have evaded consultation by labelling changes as temporary even though the Department of Health guidelines concede that temporary changes can result in 'a substantial variation' of services and should not then be exempt from consultation processes. Neither is there any definition of either 'temporary' or 'substantial' in legislative provisions. It is the health authorities themselves who now determine what is to be considered a 'substantial variation' in the use of hospital buildings or the closure of services for the purposes of consultation.

Several disputed variations in service have given rise to applications for judicial review where it has been alleged that consultation requirements have not been fully complied with. But further restraint is placed on CHC effectiveness by their being unable to take legal action on their own behalf or on behalf of those they

---

68   HSC(IS)207.

represent. Litigation has so far failed to bring about any revision of either guidelines or actual consultation procedures, with the result that the influence of CHCs on service variations tends to be marginal and rearguard, despite taking up a disproportionate amount of resources and time. The impotence of CHCs and the deficiency of current consultation provisions was clearly demonstrated in a recent case where the RHA failed to consult the relevant CHC regarding a decision to close and relocate a bone marrow unit at which a two year old child was due to receive treatment.[69] The child's father sought judicial review on the grounds of failure to consult the CHC on a substantial variation in service. Despite this being upheld by the court, no declaration of unlawfulness or order to quash the decision was granted. As the unit had already relocated the court considered that such an action would be of no benefit and therefore pointless.

As regards statutory provisions, time allowed for the formal consultation period is often too short to enable a thorough examination of the all issue. This is aggravated by the fact that plans may be changed without allowing for further examination and comment. Any need to submit all comments received on proposed changes to the relevant CHC for a final response has been dropped. Nor is there any obligation to repeat the consultation process unless any revised proposals are so different that they constitute fresh ones. The question whether the revised proposals are sufficiently different to warrant fresh consultation is essentially a matter of degree. Further, where the health authority is satisfied that in the interest of the health service a decision has to be taken without allowing time for consultation there is no obligation to do so.[70]

Similar criticisms to those made in regard to substantial variations in health services have been made of Trust application consultation processes. The period for consultation was again only three months and public meetings were left to the discretion of the relevant RHAs and Trust applicants. The organisation of ballots of the proposed Trust employees was specifically excluded from the consultation process. The reason given for this was that ballots were thought unlikely to assist the Secretary of State in assessing the impact of the proposal on local services or the ability of management to run the proposed Trust. This contrasted sharply with consultation and ballot requirements for the opting out of schools from local education authority control under the Education (Reform) Act (1988). Under ss 60, 61 of that Act a secret ballot of parents must be held and individuals have a right to object to

---

69   *R v North West Thames RHA ex p Daniels* (1994) 19 BMLR 67.

70   (1985) Regulations para 19(2).

the Minister if a proposal to 'opt out' of local authority control is forwarded to him. In addition the governing bodies of grant maintained schools must include a number of parent governors, to represent the consumer interest. This too contrasts with the public representation provisions Trust boards.

It is also significant that the statutory consultation provisions regarding Trust applications had to be triggered only after plans were crystallised and a great deal of energy and resources had been expended. Amongst the eight key factors on which Trust applications have been required to focus in order to obtain the approval of the Secretary of State are the 'overall aims of the trust and the benefits for the patients and the local community' and 'the way in which services will be developed and quality assured'. These are obviously matters about which the public as consumers either individually or collectively might have an interest and might wish to express a view.

Research carried out into the fulfilment of consultation requirements for Trust applications were enlightening.[71] Many Trust applications had the appearance of promotional brochures rather than consultation documents and attributed to trust status not only a number of benefits which would have accrued in any case but quality attainments which could be achieved in any unit by good management. Financial information was seen as optimistic and inadequate and there were also considerable gaps in the consultation documents, although these subsequently provided some opportunity for campaigning. In addition, the availability of the full consultation documents varied greatly, although most applicants provided summary leaflets for wider circulation. There was also a gap in consultation in regard to voluntary and community groups, the CHC being relied upon to undertake this. Trent, one of the largest regions consulted with only the relevant CHC and the Local Council for Voluntary Service. As a result only four responses were received. Yorkshire region on the other hand consulted widely and received over 3,000 replies from individuals and organisations. If CHCs were to be relied on to promote extensive consultation this should have been discussed and organised in advance and adequate resources should have been provided.[72]

In retrospect it appears that the effort that went into opposing trust status was not worth it. The decisions made bore no relation to the comments or protests made. The few trust applications rejected by the

---

71 Hogg and Martin, *The Future of Consultation in the NHS* (GLACHC, 1993).
72 *ibid*.

Secretary of State appeared unrelated to staff or community views or the amount of local lobbying.

The new role forged for DHAs, that of 'champion of the people'[73] has had significant implications for CHCs, and public consultation as health authorities have been encouraged to develop links with local resident and community groups. This consumer advocate function of DHAs has provided a challenge which has entailed changes to DHA philosophy and culture, which many health authorities have done their best to meet. But it is important to recognise that the means by which DHAs have built up 'healthy alliances' have been crucial to the establishment of public input to health care planning and the future viability of both health authority and CHC roles. In the process of setting up community panels and forums it would have been sensible for DHAs to provide resources to CHCs so that the latter's skills, knowledge and expertise were neither duplicated nor lost. Community Health Councils although perhaps an imperfect player should be enabled to play a key role in the continual development of a system which could aid the proper identification of shared interests and provide wider public input into policy.

Although the opportunity exists to ensure effective representation and appraisal of all relevant interests, much depends on health authorities being prepared to be innovative about devising arrangements and open in their conduct. In reality it is extremely difficult for health authorities to adopt a role of reconciling the potentially varying views about what is needed for the locality. The development of alliances might have mitigated to some extent the danger which some DHAs have felt that as institutions they are vulnerable to criticism from all quarters and has to some extent highlighted some of the informal decision-making networks which operate. But sustaining such informal connections requires a strong commitment to open and co-operative decision making and broadened access to requisite data.

In addition to the flaws apparent in the concept of collective choice in health care, the preference for consumerism and individual choice is more about customer relations than any enhanced rights which entail true partnership or power sharing.[74] The major objective of recent policy to expand the capacity of patients to act as consumers is reiterated in the inclusion of health services in the Citizens Charter initiative which seeks to make public services more answerable to their

---

73 'Developing Districts' EL (90) MB/86 NHSE.
74 C Pollitt, 'Beyond the Management Model: the case for broadening performance assessment in government and public services' (1988) *Financial Accounting and Management* 2(3).

users and to raise overall quality. Under Charter principles every citizen is entitled to expect from public services explicit standards, a greater degree of openness, regular consultation and an effective complaints system. The rights and standards of the Patients Charters are designed to meet the commitments of the Citizens Charter and specifically sets out a number of guaranteed rights and a number of standards which the NHS is to achieve as 'circumstances and resources allow'.

The principles and initiative of the Citizens and Patients Charter have been welcomed but the question remains whether the Charter is delivering a better deal for the public and fulfilling the opportunity to empower them as citizens as rhetoric would have us believe. Much depends on the quality of the mechanisms and procedures developed to give substance to the Charter initiative and the significance attached to those procedures by those responsible for their implementation and monitoring. Whilst none of the Charter principles actually amount to legal rights, failure by health bodies to comply with the Patients Charter falls within the investigative scope of the Health Service Ombudsman.[75]

Presently the Charter appears to be reinforcing the patient only as a consumer with very limited and indirect capacity to influence policy decisions. The overall tenor of the Charter is primarily one of individual rights in the doctor-patient relationship and an emphasis on individualised aspects of choice. Many of the provisions of the Patients Charter are hardly new. Taken with other gaps in NHS democratic processes the public is likely remain remote or even entirely absent from crucial decisions on the actual supply and delivery of services.

Openness

One of the key factors for the exercise of choice either collectively or individually is to ensure that information is available at a time and in a form that optimises its usefulness. This is currently constrained by both managerial and governmental operational philosophy which has traditionally tended towards confidentiality.

The central prerequisite for genuine choice at the collective and individual level is clearly openness, a transparency which needs to embrace all decision-making from policy setting through implementation to monitoring. A commitment to openness is of prime importance in order to counteract the tendency of organisations to control and distort information which might in turn prevent issues

---

75   For example *Airdale NHS Trust*. Case E 867/93-94 HC 545 pp 172–80.

being the subject of proper debate and reduce capacity for reasoned choices to be made about priorities and resource distribution.

In June 1995 the NHSE introduced a Code of Practice on Openness into the NHS as a response to the government's commitment in the White Paper on Open Government,[76] to ensure greater access by the public to information about public services. The Code covers health authorities, NHS Trusts, the Mental Health Act Commission and Community Health Councils and complements the Code of Access to Information which applies to the Department of Health and NHSE. The Code was prepared with the guidance of a steering group, chaired by the NHSE Director of Corporate Affairs with membership drawn from the NHS and other relevant organisations. A draft Code was launched for consultation for a period of 10 weeks by the Secretary of State in September 1994.

The draft Code was generally criticised for lacking clarity, for being too cautious and defensive and for its negative expression, concentrating too much on information that should not be divulged rather than the promotion of a new culture of openness. Critics pointed out that no information should be out of bounds unless patient confidentiality is under threat. In other words, there should be a presumption in favour of disclosure, unless there are sound and explicit reasons to the contrary. The issue of charging for information was also contentious. The draft Code also left too much discretion for its interpretation to health service organisations and failed to tackle one of the fundamental concerns raised, namely the procedures for appointment to health authority and trust boards.

What eventually emerged displays some improvement on the initial draft, but as with the Patients Charter there is little that is new. Taken with the Codes of Conduct and Accountability, the Code on Openness is a welcome step towards transparency which the public clearly have a right to expect in the governance of a public service. However, the Code represents a shallow step rather than any great leap forward as weaknesses and flaws remain.

The stated aims of the Code are to ensure that people:

- have access to available information about services provided by the NHS, the cost of those services, quality standards and performance against targets;

- are provided with explanations about proposed service changes and have an opportunity to influence decisions on such changes;

---

76   (1993) Cmnd 2290.

- are aware of the reasons for decisions and actions affecting their own treatment;

- know what information is available and where they can get it.

In implementing the Code the NHS must:

- respond positively to requests for information (except in circumstances identified in the Code);

- answer requests for information quickly and helpfully, and give reasons for not providing information where this is not possible;

- help the public to know what information is available so that they can decide what they wish to see and whom they should ask;

- ensure that there are clear and effective arrangements to deal with complaints and concerns about local services and access to information, and that these arrangements are widely publicised and effectively monitored.

However, arguably barriers still remain to public access to information. Although the Code lays down ground rules regarding permissible charges for information, people with legitimate interests may well be deterred. It is recommended that charging should be exceptional but is nevertheless within the discretion of the health organisation. No charge should be made for individuals enquiring about services or treatment available to them, or for inquiries form the press or other media; CHCs, MPs, local authorities or Citizens Advice Bureaux. For requests from others it is recommended that there be no charge for the first hour of time taken in dealing with them and a charge not exceeding £20 for subsequent hours.

NHS organisations are not required to make available copies of the documents or records containing the information although the Code does add that it may be simpler to do this if the documents do not contain anything other than the information requested. One or two 'enterprising' authorities have interpreted this to mean that documents may be viewed by appointment at the Chief Executive's Office!

Information which is required to be published is listed in para 5 of the Code but much of this is already publicly available, including annual reports, a summary of strategic direction documents and in the case of Trusts a summary of business plans and details of the remuneration of board members. Information which may be withheld is listed in para 9 and again leaves quite substantial discretion in interpretation to the health organisation. Both these main paragraphs are supplemented by details specific to health authorities and Trusts which are set out in the annexes to the main Code. Here three categories are identified; information which must be published, additional information which may be published as a matter of good practice and information which may be available on request. Again a great deal is left to the discretion of the health body concerned and given the past record of secrecy and tendency to categorise much material under 'commercial confidentiality', one can surmise that the Code will be marginal only in its effect. This concern is backed up by the different requirements for health authorities and Trusts. Whilst health authorities must hold all their board meetings in public subject to certain provisions regarding personnel and commercial matters, Trusts are required to hold only one public meeting a year in accessible venues and at times when the public are able to attend. The Code merely adds that public access to more general meetings or to board meetings is good practice already followed by an increasing number of Trusts.

It can also be argued that publication of audited annual accounts is too late to be of any use, and that quarterly financial reports would be preferable. Also of greater use would be publication of market testing plans, the full results of clinical audit and all waiting time including the time likely to be experienced to be placed on a waiting list.

A very noticeable difference between the draft Code and its final version is the language used. The draft Code was much more user friendly, the final Code is expressed more in what can be termed 'civil service speak' and to some extent gives an overall impression of a legal document. Whilst some criticisms of the draft have been addressed, in that there is certainly more detail, some of the main flaws have been merely couched in new terms, and their overall effect remains.

In considering accessibility to information and information systems it should be remembered that they take on different forms depending on the balance of concerns represented during the processes of their development. In the health service two main perspectives have been identified; one that is clinically led and the other that is management led. Emphasis on the latter can result in insufficient consideration being given to medical evaluation of respective services and treatments and vice versa. The main concern is that shifts in practice can be attempted through the development of information systems which fail to articulate that particular kinds of information are privileged and serve to reinforce particular and potent perspectives about what the NHS is, what its goals are and what its procedures should be.[77] Information in other words is never neutral, the values which underlie its generation not only influence responses to it but also influence

---

77 Coombs and Cooper, *Accounting for Patients; information technology and the NHS* White Paper (Centre for Research on Organisation, Management and Technological Change UMIST, 1990) 9.

awareness of alternatives and priorities. This is why more than a basic access to information is needed. To reach its full potential openness requires the specific devising of mechanisms for the actual generation of information in a form which can be effectively utilised to widen policy choices.

CONCLUSION

So what assessment can be made of the NHS reforms five years on from their beginning? In the first instant it is true to say that some inefficiencies and waste have been necessarily eradicated and management is on the whole much more accountable for expenditure. But these gains have been achieved at a price. Administrative and transaction costs, which have soared, appear to militate against any overall benefit being passed to patients.

Most clearly, the reforms have largely failed to grasp the opportunity to enhance participation in health policy by the public or their representatives. In essence the possibility of the provider market increasing choice is problematic. Statutory consultation measures remain minimal and for the most part ineffective; the classic case of 'too little, too late'. Enhanced choice has been presented as a product of competition rather than through any clear collective participation in local or national policy decisions. But competition lies only at the fringe of NHS operations and in practice there is more management than market.[78] At the same time that collective input into local level policy decisions has moved further into the shadows, individual choice has also been restricted by the contracting process, particularly in the acute sector. In many areas the local hospital Trust has a near monopoly of service provision as health authorities and GPs are not prepared to inconvenience patients by placing many contracts further afield, other than those for highly specialised care. Although a proportion of treatment is inevitably carried out in hospitals or clinics with which there is no prior contract, there is no open-ended commitment to meet all extra-contractual referrals. Indeed if there were accountability for GPs, referrals would be lost. Paradoxically the burden of ECRs may tempt health authorities to divert funds from contracts for mainstream services. Either way, choice, quality or both may be affected. The reduction in community representation, including the previous right of local authorities to appoint members to health authorities has been countered by an increased reliance placed on business expertise.

---

78   S Boyle and A Harrison (1995) HSJ.

Business skills and management expertise are of course an essential requirement for any organisation, public or private, but where essentially the consumer has little access to individual choice there needs to be a balance ensure access through collective means. Although there are some very innovative informal exercises which have sought to involve community groups and others in decisions about priorities, these have not always been reflected in purchasing patterns to any notable degree.

This gives rise to doubts as to whether local health authorities have been properly equipped to manage the networks and associations necessary to produce a coherent organisation to make difficult decisions. Mental health, care of the elderly and coronary care frequently lead as areas for funding and development. But it seems that there is an unwillingness on the part of health authorities to make hard choices. There remains a tendency to try to satisfy as many interests as possible and health authorities are uncertain how much weight to give to information from different sources. Hence, responsiveness to public needs has not always appeared to be paramount as purchasers face competing demands from the centre, providers and the community. In addition, national objectives and guarantees imposed on contracts without discussion of local implications can result in standards being demanded that are virtually unattainable. Whether the newly merged health authorities will continue to espouse the existing responsibilities of DHAs and FHSAs and their traditional contradictions, or whether there will be the possibility of innovation is open to question. The crucial point is that the influences underlying present compromises that health authorities have to make need to be explicit and the subject of scrutiny.

Competition inherently encourages collusive conduct because the latter tends to produce economies of scale, concentrates expertise and generates effective financial leverage. But none of these necessarily benefit patients in preference to health service management. The limitations of competition are thus becoming apparent in practice if not in theory. There is a risk that the alliances that are currently being formed, largely as a result of competition, will result in the values and requirements of local communities being lost and have a negative impact on choice. A process of collaboration would on the other hand reduce prevalent uncertainty and could encourage innovation and initiative. Collaboration is seen as empowering and inclusive and is argued to be the potential 'watchword of the new NHS'.[79] The Audit Commission has also pointed out that the public interest will be best

---

79 *Shared Purchasing and Collaborative Commissioning* (NAHAT, 1994).

served if the parties strive to maintain an open and co-operative style when they negotiate contracts and review performance. But this should initially require an evaluation of the possible models for co-operative purchasing and integrated planning initiatives.[80] This is no simple matter of course, collaboration needs proper structure and support, as a number of factors can conspire to either reduce or underline its effects. Ambiguous regulation or NHSE guidance, insufficient resources, institutional stagnation and professional resistance, all present a challenge to collaborative perspectives.

Furthermore, there is still a lack of adequate information on medical activity to enable purchasing, collusive, co-operative or otherwise, to operate effectively. Although data about costs is rapidly expanding, evidence based medicine and care, information about how cost effective techniques relate to outcomes is in its infancy. But research and development is not an optional extra. It is an essential ingredient which should underpin the content and delivery of care and assist clinical, managerial and policy decisions in any modern health service.[81]

Quite possibly the process of change has just begun. The reliance on the old structures is arguably inhibiting development of new ways to deliver health services. It may be that the optimal configurations for purchasers, providers, and contract models have not yet been reached. Purchasing has certainly changed the balance of power within the NHS and all kinds of boundaries are shifting and becoming blurred; especially those between primary and secondary care and health and social care. But there are no blue prints or framework for this reworking of relationships between health authorities, GPs and providers. At the same time the patterns of *provision* of health services have hardly altered. There is perhaps a real need now to look at more innovative ways to deliver care. There have been suggestions that speciality Trusts which deliver a particular service based on a number of providers rather than within the confines of a physical facility should be developed to facilitate a seamless web of different kinds of care.[82] There are also sound arguments for local government authorities for taking on much of the purchasing of role of health to better integrate health with other related services. This would not only improve local accountability but could enhance the possibility of

---

80 *ibid.*

81 A new programme is in place within the Research and Development Directorate in the NHSE which is designed to evaluate developments in science and technology.

82 These might be disease or client group based, eg oncology services or care of the elderly. Others have suggested occupational group Trusts eg psychology or radiotherapy which contract widely for services.

shifting provision of care from the acute sector to more community responsive clinics. There are already a number of joint commissioning initiatives for some community services such as learning disabilities and mental health, as well as other aspects of health and social care, but anything further would probably require close consideration, not to mention further legislation.

In conclusion, public effectiveness in countering what are currently and primarily management perspectives of health care and in participating in policy decisions in the NHS is likely to continue to tend towards tokenism unless supported by an institutional framework that is procedurally structured to ensure that the public interest is properly taken into account.

CHAPTER 5

THE ART OF GOVERNANCE

Although the debate about the suitability of markets and competition and the role of regulation in public policy-making is likely to continue in many quarters it is quite clear that we are in a new era in terms of the delivery of government services. It has become increasingly obvious and important that governments concentrate their energies on taking a strategic role. Standards and principles may be set centrally, but government cannot possibly possess the information necessary to manage effectively throughout regions and local communities. But that being the case we must ensure that the widespread developments taking place in the public sector do not undermine the fundamental requirements of choice and accountability. In the UK public law has been particularly deficient in keeping pace with the reforms and is consequently unable adequately to oversee the conduct of the unelected bodies, 'the disconcerting number of quangos', that have come to be effecting government policy in recent years.[1] Nor does it give adequate support either to consultation or the provision of information. Hence in the British setting the process of communication that should take place in an advanced democracy between the government and the governed is weak. In seeking to correct this the aim should be to search for effective means in combining value for money with choice which underline basic human and social rights. This may be easier said than done but it presents a challenge that is unlikely to be avoided.

In contrast to other policy areas and perhaps contrary to popular belief actual 'marketisation' of the core of health care is making only slow headway. This is most probably due to inherent restraints within the nature of health care itself which is acknowledged to display certain traits which militate against the market operating an equitable and efficient allocation of resources. The evidence of this is there to see in a number of countries, even the United States. Governments are involved in varying but mostly predominant degrees in the regulation of health care in a number of dimensions; in terms of access, in terms of the organisation of finance, and in controlling delivery. Markets are only tentatively moving out from the margins of health where the

---

1   J Stewart, *Ego Trip* (Democratic Audit, 1992).

competitive delivery of certain services such as optics, pharmaceuticals and the contracting out of cleaning, catering and laundry has been less contentious.

In spite of this in the UK and New Zealand, the overall assumption remains that any 'imperfections' of market operations can be 'ironed out'. The ideology is that competition, will stimulate the development of a system which would have the economic incentive and organisational capability to limit unnecessary services and develop new efficient patterns of care. There is also an assumption that this framework will be sufficiently flexible to accentuate different values and combinations of service that will accord with the needs and wishes of purchasers and consumers. The optimum means of containing costs, increasing efficiency, improving quality and enhancing consumer sovereignty over health care decisions is thus seen to be by a momentum towards pro-market and pro-competitive strategies. Consequently the governments of both countries have declared themselves to be on the long and winding track of what has come to be termed 'managed' competition. However, the above assumptions need to be carefully addressed.

MARKETS AND THE NHS

For anyone committed to equality of access, choice, accountability and improved quality in health care the initial impression gained from much of the rhetoric of the recent reforms, Citizens Charter and market literature is one of shared values and of familiar and worthy goals. On closer examination this begins to dissipate. This is because these values and goals are being constrained through a narrow perception of the possibilities for utilisation the of market concept. This is a perception that entails a bare a minimum of public involvement in decision-making and inadequate procedures for public accountability. In short, the essence of constitutional beliefs and democratic political processes are largely missing from the new structure of the NHS.

This has created tensions which are evident in the reluctance on the part of health service management to give greater rein to market strategies and the strain in 'market' regulation and guidance between that intended to encourage competition on the one hand and that intended to protect perceptions of the wider public interest on the other. It is therefore essential to ascertain under what conditions, extent and kind of competition the actual quality of care can be improved and whether or how far the operation and effects of the current 'provider or internal market' are compatible with *a priori* values; choice and accountability.[2] Should there be competition between providers only, purchasers only, or both? These are the issues and only once these questions have been addressed can a satisfactory regulatory framework be developed. From a public law perspective institutional design is a central concern and the issues that arise relate to legitimate processes for decision-making and the delivery of fundamental expectations.

Market mimicking mechanisms seek to promote the efficient use and delivery of resources and correct misallocation through competition and decisions based primarily on cost-benefit analysis. But the dynamics of competition in health care are still relatively unclear. Whilst competition may be instrumental in achieving efficiency under certain conditions, these are not usually sufficiently articulated to enable them to be incorporated into policy choices. In addition, because of the lack of any clear philosophy and concept of health services, the meanings of cost and benefit have been open to interpretation to suit different and often very narrow purposes. The resultant information, biased though it is, is then presumed to reflect the accepted, general view. Under the auspices of new public management the current approach to health care cost is most frequently understood to mean a monetary equivalent. Benefit too is regarded as a quantifiable measure of treatment outcome in terms of mortality and morbidity rates, length of stay in hospital, reduction of waiting times.

In some contexts these measures will be adequate but the purposes that justify them are rarely specified. Such statistics tend to oversimplify the way health care is experienced. We have seen that 'health' has a spectrum of meaning. Most frequently it is understood as the absence of disease and death and health care is then seen in terms of as a defence against both. On this definition particular clinical interventions can be evaluated in terms of monetary cost and in terms of the benefits of reduced disease and death rates. However, even these assessments are fraught with difficulties.

In its wider dimension of health and health care is understood as a social and caring as well as a curative activity, its goals being to promote well-being and enhance the quality of life. Although, of course, advocates of the current reforms recognise that modern health care has more than one function, some aspects, because they may be difficult to measure in any quantitative or statistical terms have been virtually excluded from cost-benefit analysis, even though such

---

2   In the USA some of the most successful schemes are those that are self-insured, self-managed statewide health insurance co-operatives, where competition operates not just on cost but quality.

matters are likely to have a considerable effect on social organisation and investment in health care provision. In other words the social evaluation aspect which can only be expressed through forms of citizen choice is absent. Until a more holistic view can be taken of the effectiveness of health policy it will be difficult to identify the effective and efficient use of resources and misallocation is likely to continue. Only in Canada, in particular Nova Scotia, has a 'health audit' of the impact decisions on health make on other fields of public policy making been advocated.

QUALITY AND EFFECTIVENESS

One of the primary means of ensuring quality is seen to be through the processes of contracting and bargaining for services between purchasers and providers. The notion is that the demands of purchasers will influence the provision of high quality care. Hospitals or other providers that continually deliver unacceptable quality will face a declining demand for their services and will be thus induced to improve their quality to recapture business. However, improvements to quality depend very much on a nexus of interlinked factors not least the ability to define and agree quality standards and the capacity to determine whether those standards are met.

Patients as ultimate consumers of health care are intended to have a role in assuring quality by virtue of exercising greater choice in provision. But, in reality there appears to be little scope for the consumer to exercise any real choice at the point of entry into health care for several reasons. The position of consumers of clinical care is widely recognised as dissimilar to that of consumers in other markets and the strategies that apply to the choice of other services or goods are only available to patients to a very limited extent. In fact there are few other areas where the consumer is so *ill-equipped* to exercise any sovereignty. Some forms of care may be sufficiently recurrent to enable certain patients to make up their own minds as to whether or not they are receiving good quality care or they may be able to rely to some extent on the experience of friends or family. But since no two episodes of clinical intervention nor any two patients, for that matter, are alike, these means carry inherent restrictions.[3]

The scarcity of accurate information inevitably plays a part in this situation. As Newdick has pointed out no measures of quality are free

---

3   T Jost, 'The Necessary and Proper role of Regulation to Assure the Quality of Health Care' (1988) *Houston Law Review* 25.

from ambiguity and the evidence which they present is equivocal.[4] There is frequently no consensus of the value of many medical practices amongst doctors themselves making it more difficult for patients who lack technical knowledge to assess adequately the quality of diagnosis and treatment and make rational choices. In addition, as most health services are required with relative speed there is a limit on the extent to which the patient can 'shop around' to find the better services.

This situation may change to some extent in the future due to the development of evidence-based medicine (EBM). Currently, EBM is beginning to make an impact on medical knowledge, policy choices and health service research programmes. However, it's ultimate impact on patient choice is less certain and its effectiveness is also open to question.[5] Whilst medical interventions logically should always be based on the best possible evidence it has been pointed out that EBM is a two edged sword. It appears to have become 'the flavour of the 1990's' for a number of reasons. First it provides a structured and systematic scientific means of knowledge which relies neither on the vested interests of the pharmaceutical industry nor traditional specialist domination and anecdotal evidence. Second it can provide a policy tool for guiding purchasing decisions and is thus useful as a control mechanism to health service management. Finally it has created a whole new market for scientific education in health, a new area of expertise which seems set to become essential to health care services. But, it has been argued that EBM also has some major limitations. Being scientific it excludes the experiences of patients and local communities. It thus allows decision making to remain professionally dominated, making implicit value judgments about effectiveness which patient choice might not reflect. It is also essentially reductionist, having a tendency to simplify complex clinical practice to consideration of 'primary diagnosis' only and those treatment outcomes that are easily quantified. It may therefore lead to a devaluation of the unquantifiable and distort understanding of that which can be quantified.[6]

Thus, even with the growth of EBM, the capacity of patients to make useful judgments about quality through their own experience and research remains, to a large extent, restricted. Individual patient choices are very much of a partnership or surrogate nature made 'on trust' either through the medical profession or through purchasing

---

4   C Newdick, *Who Should We Treat? Law Patients and Resource Allocation in the NHS* (1995) p 51.

5   'The appliance of science?' (1995) *Health Matters* Autumn p 1.

6   See *ibid* for a full explanation.

health authorities. This is an inherent assessment problem which can generate a series of dysfunctional dilemmas, uncertain objectives and limited effectiveness – a vicious circle of ambiguity.[7]

Choice is also being restricted through the contracting process. In many areas the local NHS Trust has a near monopoly of service provision. Health authorities and GP fund holders tend not to place many contracts further afield, other than those for highly specialised treatment. Although a proportion of care is inevitably be carried out in hospitals with which the health authority or GP does not have a contract, for example in cases of emergency, there is to be no open-ended commitment on the part of health authorities to meet all non-contractual referrals.[8] Even where there is no monopoly of provision there may be informal collusion between providers to limit certain services or providers may go for a 'least risk' rather than for a more comprehensive selection of services. 'Shopping around' therefore and the exercise of choice may be even less of a possibility now than it was under previous arrangements. Such evidence as there is suggests that whilst the patients of GP fundholders are benefiting choice for others has not been enhanced to any significant degree.[9] This possibility of a lack of direct consumer choice was recognised by Enthoven, the originator of the internal market concept who saw it as a major drawback.[10]

Doubts have already been expressed about the future role of Community Health Councils (CHC) in their present form as an adequate vehicle for public input into local health care provision. Although consultation and public scrutiny has been seen as particularly pertinent to the role of health authorities there has been persistent disquiet about public accountability and choice since the onset of the reforms. In the early days the Social Services Select Committee recommended that urgent consideration be given to the ways in which the views of patients could be put before those involved in the planning and delivery of care. But there has been given little formal regulatory recognition of the need for systematic consultation, although health authorities were urged to adopt a 'champion of the people' role by identifying and reflecting the views of local inhabitants throughout the purchasing process. More recently NHS Executive

---

7   R Saltman and C von Otter, *op cit* p 115.

8   This was highlighted by the recent case of 'child B' whose father sought judicial review to try to require a health authority to fund unusual and expensive treatment. See R James and D Longley, *Ex parte B and Tragic Choices*. [1995] PL 367.

9   A Mahon, D Wilkin, C Whitehouse, 'Choice of Hospital for Elective Surgery' (1994) in *GPs and Patients Views in Evaluating the NHS Reforms* (R Robinson and J le Grand Eds).

10   A Enthoven, 'Words from the source' (1985) *BMJ NHS Review* 298.

guidance has also emphasised that greater voice should be given to service users.[11]

Research suggests that whilst all health authorities are keen to stress their broad commitment to public involvement, the extent to which this commitment is translated into practice varies considerably.[12] *Voices off: tackling the democratic deficit in health*[13] indicates clearly that the reforms have not provided any mechanisms for public views to influence health choices directly and strongly recommends that health authorities investigate alternative and more effective means for involving the public in strategic decisions.[14] The report also calls for a radical overhaul of Community Health Councils (CHC) powers and review of the degree of independence between the NHS and CHCs. It further advocates a move towards more open governance of health services.

In general terms it appears that health authorities are struggling with public involvement in the relation to a number of key objectives; to inform the public about health issues and concerns; to establish accountability and credibility with local communities; and to seek feedback on current services and future needs. Health authorities it seems are uncertain about the ultimate aim of public involvement. It is regarded as far easier to develop the practice of involvement in relation to actual service users around clearly defined service-specific agendas[15] than to identify appropriate ways of engaging the wider public.

Some health authorities have begun to consider more specific mechanisms such as consumer panels, advisory groups, locality groups and liaison with voluntary organisations in order to tap into a more informed consumer voice, but these developments are generally at an early stage.[16] It seems that frequently other issues are given priority and the demands of central government skew purchasers towards superficial and short term solutions which by-pass the opportunity for the development of more substantial and ongoing public involvement such as has been evident in Nova Scotia.

As regards public involvement with providers, Trusts are under no obligation to conduct any part of their business in open meetings.

---

11 *Priorities and Planning Guidance for the NHS* (NHS Executive, 1995/6).

12 C Lupton and P Taylor, 'Coming in from the Cold' (1995) HSJ 22.

13 Institute for Public Policy Research (1995).

14 IPPR found that health authority expenditure on public involvement varied from £900–£100,000 over two years.

15 These kinds of schemes are not without problems but have been shown act as a spur to service improvements. J Bradburn 'Eye Opener' (1994) HSJ.

16 *ibid* Lupton p 23.

Neither do CHCs have an automatic right to attend routine meetings or receive documentary material relating to planning. Admission to such meetings is discretionary and has often resulted in a cloak of 'commercial confidentiality' being put around Trust activities. It follows that a great deal of information about organisation, forward planning and management objectives is not available for public comment. In place of direct access to Trust business CHCs are expected to deal with health authorities on matters relating to the provision and level of local services. But the structures for involvement are weak here too and without proper statutory backing CHCs are becoming increasingly dependent on the goodwill of health authority management.[17] Without access to information and participation as of right it requires outstanding perseverance on the part of CHCs to continue to represent the consumer diligently.

Overall it is presently too easy for the exercise of collective choice to be limited in the policy process and be based on too little information to be effective. Individual choice is then also restricted at the point of entry to health care. True partnership or power sharing would entail offering access to performance information of the sort that could be used to make the exercise of policy choices real and a framework to facilitate collective organisation and representation.[18]

CONTRACT AND CHOICE

Contract has of course always been associated with markets and choice, but it has been identified as one of the more difficult methods of public service organisation, carrying in its wake not only the need for elucidation of content, but the necessity to monitor delivery. However even though the current market concept of contract, as a means of determining what shall be produced and consumed in the public service, is insufficient to secure constitutional values,[19] there are considerable advantages to contracting for services through the provision of competitive pressures and incentives to improve services without excessive political interference. The contracting approach offers:

the possibility of greater accountability of public services by specifying objectives and delegating functions to accountable organisations with

---

17 ACHCEW Survey of CHC Relations with NHS Authorities (1991).

18 C Pollitt, 'Measuring performance of public Services; A Consumer Perspective' (1988) Leverhulme Discussion Paper.

19 N Lewis, 'How to Reinvent British Government' (1993) European Policy Forum.

separate interests. It could also provide the basis for expanding individual legal entitlement by specifying obligations of the service provider.[20]

Within the NHS the contract mechanisms is regarded as having two main advantages. It separates the role and responsibilities of purchasers of health care from that of providers and just as importantly, by setting out criteria and targets for delivery it is seen as a means of focusing both provider and purchaser attention on the quality of care and thus supplies a catalyst for improvement.

However, contract does not of itself empower individuals in the formation of policies which lie behind contracts. Consequently contracting, NHS contracts in particular, are really instruments of governance more akin to delegated legislation than the commercial variety. As such, they should be liable to constitutional assessment examination, to be open, accessible and subject to a wide variety of public input, and be monitored delivery of quality. consequently it can be argued that there is a need to develop a distinctly public law version of contract which might give these protections.

The Citizens Charter

A little has already been said about the role of Citizens Charter and Patients Charter. Building on current NHS reforms the aim of the provision and revision of Patient's Charters is to set out what the NHS should provide and what patients are entitled to expect from health services. A national Patients Charter already specifies 10 individual guaranteed 'rights':[21]

- to receive health care on the basis of clinical need, regardless of ability to pay;

- to be registered with a general practitioner;

- to receive emergency medical care at any time;

- to be referred to a consultant where necessary;

- to be given a clear explanation of any treatment proposed, including any risks and available options;

- to have access to health records (although this only applies to records made after 1 November 1991);

---

20 I Harden, *The Contracting State* (1992).
21 These are not legal rights.

- to withhold consent to treatment or participation in medical research or student training;

- to be given detailed information about local health services, including quality standards and maximum waiting times;

- to be guaranteed admission for treatment by a specific date no later than two years from the day when the patient is placed on a waiting list;

- and to have any complaint about health services investigated and to receive a prompt reply from the chief executive or general manager.

The Patients Charter has also introduced nine public service principles which again do not give rise to any entitlement but are specific standards which the NHS is expected to achieve as 'circumstances and resources' allow. These are:

- respect privacy, dignity, religious and cultural beliefs;

- provision for those with special needs, such as physical and mental handicap, to be able to use health services without difficulty;

- provision of information to relatives and friends, subject to the wishes of the patient;

- standard times waiting times for ambulance services, initial assessment of what is required in accident and emergency departments and out-patient appointments;

- less frequent cancellation of operations;

- a named qualified nurse, midwife or health visitor responsible for each patient;

- improved discharge co-ordination arrangements.

Since April 1992 health authorities have also been expected to produce local charters specific to their own services which set out and publicise the main standards of provision negotiated with hospitals and other providers. These should be widely available and prominently displayed. Although the government does not regard it to be sensible to actually set national quality standards because of variations in local circumstances, guidance has been given by the NHS Executive on the main areas in which local standards of service must be established, monitored and published to provide a consistent national basis. Guidance has also been issued on maximum waiting times for treatment and specific, timed appointments for all out patients visits. Clear information about primary health care services should also be available, each general practice being required to detail the services offered.

The principles and initiative of the Citizens and Patients Charter are noteworthy and have considerable potential. But information about NHS performance against Charter standards is patchy. Government reports have failed to mention progress in attainment in a number of rights and standards,[22] and league tables on hospital performance have been even more selective.

There are therefore a number of general principles which need to be observed if the Patient Charters are to be effective in improving services in both hospitals and in general practice. Charters must become part of an overall quality programme and part of a wider policy and strategy to involve patients and the local community in decision-making. This includes the integration of clinical audit with the perceptions of patients and carers.[23]

Hogg has indicated that a framework for dialogue about how services link with each other or with other hospital departments and local authority services also needs to be established if standards are to be improved. Her research showed that users had different priorities to those set out in the Charters. The most fundamental was a concern for a reasonable standard of clinical skill and care, the second was to be treated as an individual and the third was the need for co-ordination between health and social services. Users were tired of negotiating with all agencies offering help, they wanted a service that linked practical help, treatment and care.[24] The drift of criticism was that the present focus of the Charter agenda had concentrated attention on a mechanistic view of health care; the more treatment the better, whereas most users would settle for less but better treatment. She concluded that involving users in planning and evaluating services required commitment, expertise and resources and the national framework would do better to focus on the process rather than the actual setting and monitoring of standards.

In terms of standards the NHS plays a full part in the Chartermark scheme which is intended to denote quality in services. CHCs are inevitably involved in local monitoring of standards, in publicising Charter standards and in assisting patients to enforce their rights. The Association of CHCs in England and Wales (ACHCEW) argues that it would be therefore be logical for CHCs to be consulted on the awarding of Chartermarks and to be able to nominate health services for the award. However, if the commitment to 'independent validation of performance against standards' is a serious one additional resources

---

22   H Bayley, 'Charter Challenge' (Sept 1994) HSJ.
23   C Hogg, 'Different Strokes' (May 1994) HSJ.
24   C Hogg, 'Beyond the Patients Charter; working with users' (1994) *Health Rights*.

need to be made available to CHCs.[25] NHS reforms have already been made increasing demands on CHC resources but no increases in funding have been forthcoming.

WHAT OUGHT TO BE DONE?

The NHS like other public organisations has tended to look increasingly to technical and professional solutions to its difficulties. At the same time its mechanisms for public choice and accountability have failed to adapt to these changes, leaving the way open for incremental and reactive conduct based on an inadequate analysis and superficial debate of options. Working for Patients itself was a compromise solution in which a variety of market oriented initiatives were superimposed on the existing centrally dominated, hierarchical structure of the UK health service. This has down-graded both democratic participation in policy choices and the influence of local communities. It has adopted almost exclusively financial as opposed to political or participatory criteria for goal setting and advancement.

The danger of this current direction is that consideration of outcomes will be nothing more than superficial and information systems will remain based on simple criteria, focused mainly on quantifiable results and largely unconcerned with institutional processes and the dynamics of provider-purchaser relations except as they are influenced by economic incentives. Consequently the health market is likely to be dominated by short term concerns.

Of course, it is possible to argue that the balance of power within the NHS has been adapting or shifting internally, but it is health authority and Trust management and to some extent GP fundholders who have had their scope of control extended by the processes of contracting and of management defined efficiency and effectiveness. None of this has improved the opportunity of patients to exercise their preferences either collectively or individually. Patients are to a large extent dependent on management good intentions and judgment to secure adequate and timely services. Patient concerns about policy and quality generally have no independent standing and are not incorporated automatically into health organisations choices and processes.

When the long traditions of professional dominance and public ineffectiveness are properly considered the chances of success of the *present* market approach adjusting the balance between providers or

25   *Survey of CHC Relations with NHS Authorities* (ACHCEW, 1991).

purchasers and the consumer appear unlikely. This makes the need for alternative conceptions of the market and regulation of public services and the means of their facilitation critical. It is important to note that the particular forms of management and the brand of consumerism which have recently been infused into our public institutions have not yet been demonstrated to be superior anywhere. The aim should be to develop a *brand or form* of management that takes into account the fundamental needs of public service which rest on a firm belief in the importance of a proper constitutional underpinning for all public activity.

At this fundamental level freedom of expression and choice is essential to self-fulfilment and well being. At the political level, because, by its very nature public power is exercised on behalf of all citizens, everyone has a right to participate in and express concern with its application. The challenge for society and the designers of its public institutions is to provide a means to draw together and manage those diverse and sectional interests so as to safeguard the citizen as an individual and as a member of society from arbitrary decisions. This goes much deeper than meeting the requirements and wishes of the consumer at a superficial or rhetorical level. It is more about making services accessible to choice at all levels, enhancing equity and public accountability. It is not argued here that there should be a radical reversal of current developments in health care, but it is essential that their shortcomings as well as their virtues are constantly examined. The reliance on competition between *providers* has proved to be politically and technically difficult to implement in the UK and has been further complicated by the establishment of GP fund-holders who are themselves in competition with health authorities.

Misplaced competition?

Proposed solutions to the dilemmas created by the reforms need to be feasible in health service terms as well as politically acceptable. The question is how to empower individuals to redress the decision-making balance and ensure greater opportunity to express choice and influence the conditions under which health care is provided and experienced. It has been argued that choice has both a collegiate (voice) and individual (exit) dimension.[26] In the past the preferred mechanism has often been the enhancement of 'voice' through the incorporation of the public directly into local decision-making by supplementing representative democratic power.

---

26 A Hirschman, *Exit, Voice and Loyality: responses to decline in firms, organisations and states* (1970).

This element is certainly inadequate in the new NHS. The Association of Metropolitan Authorities (AMA) recently presented a discussion document[27] which recommended that local authorities take on the role of purchasing acute services, community health services including chronic care for mental and long term illness and public health and health promotion services on behalf of residents. This has much to recommend it; not only would local democracy and accountability be enhanced but it would assist the development of a co-ordinated 'seamless web of services' which would go a long way to overcoming current fragmentation between primary, secondary and tertiary provision. The latter has encouraged 'cost shunting' whereby the policies and practices of one organisation inflict unplanned, additional expenditure on another.[28]

But whilst political empowerment may occur in these circumstances, individual influence, the lowest level of subsidiarity needs to be maintained, otherwise the individual will remain relatively powerless. The key of self fulfilment is to provide the degree of autonomy over public goods that there is over private sector consumption and to supplement the indirect form of political influence with a more direct individual wielding of choice which more nearly reflects individual preferences and experiences.

In the public sector markets and choice have been steadily criticised and held largely to correspond to exit, and therefore neither feasible nor politically acceptable as health care is not something which can be readily exited from. But choice does not have to correspond to total exit as it can be argued that an effective mechanism for enhancing individual influence over health is that of 'lateral re-entry'. Choice in this sense is equated with equal opportunity as the *patient* can choose from a number of 'health packages'. Where this is facilitated within an existing public system it will be likely to be politically acceptable. Within the publicly operated service there therefore needs to be properly designed competition which can provide an appropriate vehicle through which to revitalise existing health services.

The present UK and New Zealand model tends to run contrary to this; efficiency is closely allied to managerial decision-making, the core assumption being that improvements in performance will best be gained by management control over both the provider (supply) and patient (demand) sides of health service provision, which the health authority is expected to balance. But in the alternative form of market

---

27 *Local Authorities and Health Services; the future role of local authorities in the provision of health services* (1994).

28 For example the closure of long term care beds in the NHS has shifted the responsibility onto local authority social service departments.

mimicking strategy mentioned above, dubbed 'public competition', the patient, rather than the manager at health authority level, is the prime agent of change. This is because this latter model harnesses patient choice on the *demand* side of the economic equation in that the patient is free to choose both physician and treatment site.[29] This is much closer to the model of health care organisation in operation in Canada. Public competition entails a lesser emphasis on the capacity of managers to enhance efficiency. Instead, patient preference 'triggers a co-ordinated pattern of budgetary and personnel related incentives for improved efficiency as well as effectiveness' which operates within a defined framework of supply options which are publicly funded and which operate on the basis of explicit commitments about the appropriate characteristics of service provision.[30]

Within the NHS one possible direction to take to resolve entrenched difficulties would be to instigate competition between purchasers, not just providers, by allowing free movement between them. Purchasers would need to be funded on a new basis, for example by use of a specific form of 'voucher' or similar scheme, which could cover primary and secondary care. Services would still be free at the point of entry but money would follow the patient who would be able to choose between packages offered by purchasing organisations best to suit their needs. Once patients had a real opportunity to shift allegiances purchasers and providers would be forced to become more responsive. Patients would find themselves taken more seriously than in an exclusively voice environment.

But as competition alone is insufficient to maintain quality improvements, purchasers would need to be regulated and monitored to ensure a minimum standard which might vary for different settings and circumstances. Such a development has a possibility of exerting real pressure on costs and to some extent the problems of reconciling the accountability needs of a centrally funded organisation with those of a service whose provision is essentially local could be reduced.

NEWER PUBLIC MANAGEMENT

Recent debate about the nature of public management has aimed to clarify and expand its definition and to find a concept which successfully encompasses the distinctive elements of a public organisation. Management has been defined generally as taking

---

29 R Saltman and C Von Otter *Planned Markets and Public Competition* (Open University Press, 1992) for an explanation of 'lateral re-entry' and 'public competition' pp 84–85 and Part II.

30 *ibid* p 87.

responsibility for the performance of a system. This is stated to include 'all phases of the policy process and their co-ordination to achieve overall policy purposes'.[31]

The role of public managers is to develop a capacity to cope effectively with ambiguities, conflicts and potential instability of organisations and to recognise that accountability procedures are operated, implemented and sometimes manipulated by those within the system. This requires training and a re-orientation of the perceptions of present management objectives. Effective public management can then be defined in terms of innovativeness, adaptability, and a capacity to learn and manage change.[32] Stress is laid on management as a responsive, flexible and adaptive process which can develop a range of options for both system enabling and system maintenance functions.

In an organisation where management involves matters which stem from public purposes, values and conditions, these skills must be set against a constitutional backcloth. The task is to 'support citizenship and government'.[33] There can be no doubt that it is possible to motivate the wider public interest in this process – Canada has shown that much depends on the spirit in which the issues are approached and presented. This form of public management is central to the art of governance and requires an interactive approach where service priorities are set jointly, attempting to meet public preferences as well as professional objectives and responsibilities. Such an approach would openly formulate the problems as well as the solutions and seek to ensure that the use of markets in health care reinforced rather than undermined the broader social objectives which form the conceptual core of health services.

Additional responsiveness in policy processes could be encouraged by several means. First, at central policy level processes need to be more open to subject to comment. Second, responsiveness could be increased through further development of Patients Charters to the provision of Codes of Practice to establish norms in different aspects of service. Third local level links between management, clinicians, users and other interest groups need to be institutionalised, based on the Canadian model of hospital or community health policy committees.

However, both current and future changes require a recognition that existing mechanisms for accountability and choice lack sufficient

---

31 L Metcalf and S Richards *Improving Public Management* (1987) pp 35–42.

32 S Ranson and J Stewart *Citizenship and Government; the challenge for management in the public domain* (1989) pp 19–24.

33 *ibid* p 19.

on-going systematic evaluation of health gain. Resource management and medical audit are valuable, but are limited in their application. It is important that quality be assessed independently of costs and that there is clarity in the trade-offs between the two. A shift in emphasis needs to take place. Current accountability measures and monitoring of quality tend to focus on single events, or single settings rather than episodes or continuity of care. The tendency is to divide services into neat boxes of primary, acute and tertiary provision. As economics and technology are constantly changing, the patterns of care and the linkages between the different aspects are not well made. The result is that decisions are often taken in isolation or ignorance of other important factors and policy may be ill-founded. There is no oversight group with the breadth of vision or independence to analyse data from every possible source, identify barriers to improving overall quality and make recommendations which can be fed into policy processes. Without information about costs and benefits and the effect of policies on outcomes becoming available and being shared, overall health gains are unlikely.

INDEPENDENT REVIEW

The very nature of choice and accountability dictates that the initiative must be held by those who are the ultimate beneficiaries of public services. That initiative relies ultimately on the independent generation of information. Whilst health authorities are bodies with a potential for generating debate, testing critical assumptions and providing an opportunity to make creative use of planning evaluation, because of their many competing interests and allegiances they cannot be relied upon to respond effectively to consumer or more correctly citizen concerns. As the NHS becomes more fragmented and pluralistic, and the division between public and private provision becomes blurred, the latter requires an intermediary body to perform a less diverse role between providers and users. CHCs with an expanded remit such as that enjoyed by Canada's Provincial Health Councils are already admirably placed to fulfil the task locally.

But at parliamentary level also careful consideration should be given to the range of constituencies required to act as public watchdog both for and through Parliament. It has long been pointed out that the gaps in current accountability mechanisms and evaluative arrangements for public services beg the need for some independent assessment machinery that will have relevance for decisions on national policies. There have been a number of suggestions that intermediary advisory bodies could be specifically placed both to report to Parliament and be consulted by it and which can take an overall view of what is required.[34]

What is really being advocated is the development of quality control measures for decision-making and policy choices. Because of the limitations of budget, personnel, time and the relationship between the different NHS management bodies there can be no opportunity (nor should there be) to develop in-house all the information and specialised experience needed to make effective insights and non-biased judgments. Peters points out that public organisations have a tendency to create a 'trained incapacity' to respond in other than a single way to particular problems and issues and take other than a narrow perspective of the trade-offs involved in making critical choices.[35]

The use of an advisory body, outside the executive and capable of spanning the area of potential conflicts between medical, management and social requirements is a possible solution to the problem of presenting more diverse views and perspectives to the public and to Parliament. However, the usefulness of advisory committees may be limited where extensive amounts of data must be gathered and basic research undertaken as in the case of health policy and standard setting.[36] Although there are a considerable number of institutions which carry out research in the health care field it has often been difficult to co-ordinate and link their work. As McLachlan has stated:

> what we should be seeking are the continuing means for objective judgment on health care arrangements and policies.[37]

Klein has also pointed to the uncertainty of health policy and the importance of devising organisational structures that can readily adapt to rapidly changing circumstances. In doing so he too underscores the organisation of health care provision as a learning process. Policy judgments and parliamentary assessments therefore need to be based on comprehensive and informed evaluation. Communication is the key. To this end the establishment of an Institute of Health has been canvassed and is worthy of serious consideration.

This would be a body with a wider remit than the Clinical Standards Advisory Group (CSAG) which was established at the insistence of the House of Lords, to allay the fears of the royal colleges that clinical standards might suffer through the operation of the

---

34 I Harden and N Lewis, *The Noble Lie: the British constitution and the rule of law* (1986) and G McLachlan *What Price Quality; the NHS in Review* (1990).

35 B Guy Peters *op cit*.

36 Note the demise of the NHS Health Policy Board and the Public Health Commission in New Zealand.

37 McLachlan *op cit* p 207.

'internal market'. The key function of the CSAG is to 'provide advice on the standards of clinical care for, and access to, and availability of services to national health service patients'.[38] The House of Lords envisaged the body as having a wide remit to advise, carry out studies and submit reports on issues relating to standards of care at national, regional and local levels at the request of the Minister.

The Group's programme is decided with the Secretary of State, taking into account suggestions by health authorities and other organisations such as the royal colleges. Whilst doubts were initially expressed about the independence of the CSAG and the extent and interpretation of its powers it has questioned the efficacy of competition in its reports regarding services provided for the rarer conditions.[39] It has been suggested that since government responses to these reports have been positive the CSAG will have an important role to play in ensuring managerial strategies will not obstruct the quality of care to patients.[40] However in order to be truly independent and set a new standard of public accountability the CSAG would need to include non-professional representatives and have additional powers to consider wider ethical and social implications of health policy, not to mention more extensive resources.

McLachlan has suggested that the Institute of Medicine of the National Academy of Sciences in Washington DC (IOM) could provide a model whose form and objectives could be adapted to British purposes. The Institute was set up to try to clarify and offset problems which were being experienced in the United States in the provision of health care because of increasingly heavy demands on health services *and* their complex relations with other sectors of public policy. Recognising that the problems of health care and service delivery are so large that their solution requires the competence and concern of disciplines other than medicine the Institute is broadly based. Its 500 active members are elected from health, medical and biological sciences and other related fields such as behavioural and social sciences, administration, law and engineering. In operation it is an apolitical body capable of objective analysis of issues for recommending policy in all aspects of health care and its delivery. Members and non-member experts serve on committees for the study of critical health issues, without compensation. The issues which the Institute addresses may be identified by Congress, the executive, various foundations and other private sector organisations or by the

---

38 1990 Act s 62(1).

39 *Cystic Fibrosis* (1993) and *Neonatal Intensive Care* (1993) CSAG HMSO.

40 C Newdick *op cit.*

IOM itself. The IOM is governed by an elected council of 21 members and is organised into operating divisions dealing with health sciences policy, health promotion and disease prevention, health care services, mental health and behavioural medicine and international health. The IOM oversees a programme of some 60–70 research projects at any given time.

Within the United Kingdom health care field there is a need for a similar institution to stimulate open debate and rational learning processes by harnessing and co-ordinating existing and potential resources, and acting as a clearing house for the gathering and dissemination of information. Such a body should have a capacity to proffer advice on health policies with a fresh perspective and equally provide an independent evaluation of the impact of those policies. It would also provide a measure of public participation as public values are tightened and cemented during the processes of analysis and comment.

However the establishment of an Institute of Health or other similar organisation is by itself no guarantee of open debate and genuine accountability without supplements to Parliamentary procedures through a stronger commitment to freedom of information to open up and place on record major issues of health policy choices. 'Policy making must be observed by arc light and not by lightning'.[41]

A CONSTITUTIONAL APPROACH TO GOVERNANCE

The 'tragic choices' of health policy are inherently ethical in nature, based primarily on value rather than fact and operate in a field of palpable uncertainty. Because values are involved there may be several reasonable policy alternatives which might be adopted from any given set of circumstances. Similarly the criteria used in making these choices – issues of risk, costs and benefits, effectiveness are difficult to ascertain and subject to a number of alternative interpretations. Consequently such criteria can carry unarticulated values which shape priorities, influence perceptions of problems and feasibility of solutions.

A central feature of governance is the necessity to make choices whether at the level of 'macro' policy, which is intended to apply across the range of circumstances, or the 'micro' individual case. At both these levels and through the spectrum of those in between the choices made are affected and guided by all manner of factors. Even though reliance may be attached to regulations and guidelines different interpretations

---

41 Harden and Lewis *op cit* (1986) 303, 243.

and other principles will be applied as policy is mediated through to its implementation. Whilst governments have utilised a large variety of policy tools in recent years they have been less stringent in applying substantive principles[42] which has left our national health service bodies with too wide a discretion (not to mention the burden) regarding the values to be considered and adopted in making choices and there has been an overdose of emphasis on scientific, technological and managerial solutions. This position appears to have been avoided in Canada but not in New Zealand, consequently it seems that the former's track is the one to follow.

Market mechanisms, particularly those characterised by poor information, and an emphasis on economic accountability are unlikely to solve the major problem of the NHS which is that of producing an equitable, high quality and efficient service. Structured competition can in reality be nothing more that an administrative means of stretching limited resources, it should not be regarded automatically as a substitute for reasoned health care policy choices. By highlighting the essential ethical nature of choices in health against a backdrop of constitutional principles the *quality* of decision-making might be improved. Even though some promising avenues have been opened up which could point the way to improving health care there is a need to re-invigorate our faded constitutional expectations. A more constitutional approach is one that could avoid the current pitfalls of short term, often knee-jerk, responses to the current vicious circle of dilemmas. Organisations and people need to learn to be able to develop and mature. Properly designed against a background of constitutional underpinnings for public activity, law can assist all groups concerned with the provision of health care to establish their identity, resolve conflict, and set the norms of practice for an open and co-operative web of services.

---

42   Peters *op cit.*

INDEX